Papa Don't Pope

Published by Canon Press
P.O. Box 8729, Moscow, Idaho 83843
800.488.2034 | www.canonpress.com

Douglas Wilson, *Papa Don't Pope*
Copyright © 2016 by Douglas Wilson.

Cover design by James Engerbretson.
Cover image copyright CSA-Images. Used by permission.
Additional cover illustration by Forrest Dickison.
Interior layout by Valerie Anne Bost.

Printed in the United States of America.

Unless otherwise indicated, all Scripture quotations are from the King James Version. Scripture quotations marked "NKJV" are from the New King James Version®. Copyright ©1982 by Thomas Nelson, Inc. Used by permission. All rights reserved.

All rights reserved. No part of this publication may be reproduced, stored in a retrieval system, or transmitted in any form by any means, electronic, mechanical, photocopy, recording, or otherwise, without prior permission of the author, except as provided by USA copyright law.

Library of Congress Cataloging-in-Publication Data:
Wilson, Douglas, 1953- author.
Papa don't pope : why I'm not a Roman Catholic (and why the future is Protestant) / Douglas Wilson.
Moscow : Canon Press, 2016.
LCCN 2016026765 | ISBN 9781591281894 (pbk. : alk. paper)
LCSH: Protestant churches—Relations—Catholic Church. | Catholic Church—Relations—Protestant churches.
Classification: LCC BX4818.3 .W535 2016 | DDC 280/.042—dc23
LC record available at https://lccn.loc.gov/2016026765

16 17 18 19 20 21 22 23   12 11 10 9 8 7 6 5 4 3 2

PAPA DON'T POPE

DOUGLAS WILSON

canonpress
Moscow, Idaho

To the memory of Martin Marprelate,
who has probably never had a book dedicated to him.

CONTENTS

Introduction..ix

SECTION 1: UNITY

I: A Protestant Vision for Unity 3
II: Love the One You're With 13
III: The Ultimate Letter to Rome 21

SECTION 2: HARMONY

IV: A Work of High Harmony..................... 35
V: Authority and Apostolic Succession 43
VI: Personal Judgment........................... 57
VII: Becoming Hindu in Beverly Hills............. 73
VIII: Authority and Clarity 81

SECTION 3: THEOLOGY INCARNATED

IX: Four Kinds of Idolatry 93

X: Take the Blue Pomegranates, for Example 105

XI: Let's Go Kiss Us Some Icons 121

XII: As the Ankle Bracelet Gets Itchy 127

XIII: Theology with the Chambermaid 135

XIV: Heavenly Prayer Requests 143

XV: Corporate Testimony 147

SECTION 4: CATHOLIC FUNDAMENTALISM

XVI: Calvin's Fundamentalism 159

XVII: The Real Action is Elsewhere 163

XVIII: All Over the Map 169

XIX: Christ in the Participles 173

XX: The Smell of Boiling Water 177

Conclusion: Loyalty As Grace 181

Introduction

Given what Solomon said about no end to the making of books (Eccl. 12:12), adding yet another one might seem to require an explanation. This is particularly the case when the book concerned is a theological demarcation, seeking to set down clear lines of distinction between a classical Protestant vision of theology and the church and a Roman Catholic understanding. Don't we have enough disagreements in the world already?

Well, yes, we do have plenty of disagreements; we are running a surplus. But we do not yet have nearly enough *clear* disagreements. Before we can move from disagreement to agreement, there is an in-between step of making the disagreements plain. If we simply jump from one to another, or attempt to fix everything with an ecumenical group hug, we run the risk of sewing a new patch on an old garment with the result of just making everything worse (Mk. 2:21). This, by the way, was not a three-ingredient mixed metaphor; it was rather three metaphors condensed *seriatim*.

There are catholic reasons for expressing disagreement, in other words. I am not interested in just being disagreeable, and I see no future in stirring up mud. The church where I am privileged to labor confesses the Apostles' Creed on a weekly basis and, that being the case, every week we all say we believe in the "holy catholic church." Consequently, in publishing a book like this, I wanted to make sure that it was understood at the outset that there is a plain, and very catholic intention behind it. Put another way, true catholicity begins with defining catholicity.

So why write a book like this? Of course, one reason would be to address the particular topics outlined in the various chapters—personal interpretation, apostolic succession, *sola Scriptura*, and so on. But there is a larger reason for it, a reason behind the particular differences over particular doctrines. For the modern mind, the word *Protestant* conjures up images of protests, and for us that means marches, placards, chants, and so on. It makes you think of a group of the theologically disgruntled, united only by what they are *against*. But the original use of the word *Protestant* came from an appeal at the Diet of Speyer in 1529. An accommodation had been made for the evangelical believers just a few years earlier, and as it happened Charles V was seeking to put a stop to that accommodation. The princes who were supportive of the Reformation appealed to him not to do this. Here is one of the things they said in that appeal:

> "We are resolved, with the grace of God, to maintain the pure preaching of God's holy Word, such as is contained in the biblical books of the Old and New Testaments, without adding anything to it that may be contrary to it. This word is the only truth; it is the sure rule of all doctrine and of all life, and can never fail or deceive us. He who builds on this foundation shall stand against all the powers of hell, while all the human vanities that are set up against it shall fall before the face of God."[1]

My hope is that by reading this book, some might catch a vision of that original Protestant

---

1 Quoted by Joel Beeke, "The Protest at Speyer," *Leben Magazine* 4, no. 4 (Oct.–Dec. 2008): 9 (http://www.leben.us/volume-4-volume-4-issue-4/266-the-protest-at-speyer).

"protestimony," for that is where it all begins. To affirm certain things certainly entails denying their contraries, but a healthy spiritual movement must always begin with the affirmations. The Reformation was just that sort of positive movement of the gospel, and it is my hope to keep that reality in view even while we discuss the doctrines that such affirmations might exclude.

This kind of clarity is also very helpful in a day when classical Protestants frequently find themselves on the same side of cultural battles as devout Catholics are—say, on the right to life or on the issues swirling around the homosexual agenda. But there still remains a difference between allies and co-belligerents. Allies are fighting against the same enemy you are, and largely for the same reasons. Co-belligerents are fighting against the same enemy, but for reasons that differ, sometimes wildly. Just the other day I had a brief and very enjoyable moment of fellowship on the sidewalk of our small town. A traditionalist Catholic named Judith stopped me with, "Excuse me, are you Doug Wilson?" I indicated *yes*, never quite sure how these things are going to go. She introduced herself, and said that she generally doesn't get on with Calvinists, but all this homosexual business was *terrible*. She apparently appreciated a stand I had taken on same sex mirage in our local paper. It is my conviction that working through the issues in this book will help Protestants and Catholics work together in those areas where they *can* work together. Good fences make good neighbors.

We can know, for example, that when the pope says something entirely reasonable in the teeth of the secular establishment, we ought to agree with it. It is important to understand that we are agreeing *materially*—on the subject under discussion. But there may well be a formal element in there (his understanding of papal authority) that we must reject even while we applaud the contents of his statement.

This is related to the next obvious question. Who is this book for? The book is intended for anyone with honest questions about any of the topics addressed. That might include both decided Protestants and wobbly ones, with the same kind of breakdown on the Roman Catholic side of things. In short, I want to write about these topics for anyone interested in reading about them—and I suspect there are more than a few in that category.

Of course, a word must be said about the title *Papa Don't Pope*. What is it supposed to mean? "Papa" is what my grandkids call me, and "poping" is what happens when someone swims the Tiber, as they say. But as this book makes plain, that is hardly likely. And the phrase also riffs off that old Madonna song, "Papa Don't Preach." So the best explanation is that we were horsing around at Canon one day some months ago when somebody said that, and it stuck. You kind of had to have been there. The details are foggy, and so we have to ask you to trust us. It was funny at one time.

The book has obvious limitations, beyond those created by virtue of having been written by me. The Reformation began almost five hundred years ago, and built a great civilization in the course of its development over the subsequent centuries. Issues related to its theological foundations are obviously enormous. This is a tiny book, a pamphlet really, and makes no pretense of covering the subjects I am addressing in any kind of exhaustive depth. But while it cannot be exhaustive, and did not try to be, my hope is that it *can* be suggestive. I pray that it might help some who read it to mark out some lines for fruitful future discussion.

Classical Protestants tend to say *soli Deo gloria*. Roman Catholics might prefer *ad maiorem Dei gloriam*. May God hasten the day when we can all say amen to both.

…

SECTION 1

UNITY

CHAPTER I

A Protestant Vision for Unity

The vexed question of church unity is like the woman in the gospels—the more the physicians treat her, the worse she seems to get. In large measure, this is because church leaders (naturally enough) tend to place the locus of unity in *government*. But we need to reexamine this. Of course, governmental unity among all Christians is certainly to be desired, but is it the foundation of all unity or an instrument that will be used by God to advance that unity? Is governmental unity the foundation or the final fruit of a biblical striving toward unity? Fortunately, the Bible tells us where to look for the answers to these questions.

The same Paul who tells us to labor to maintain the unity of the Spirit in the bond of peace also tells us the *basis* of that unity. He tells us that we as Christians are to walk in a manner worthy of our calling as Christians (Eph. 4:1). Our demeanor in this is to be one of humility and patience (v. 2). With this attitude, we are equipped to obey his next command, which is the command to endeavor to keep the unity of the Spirit in the bond of peace (v. 3). This unity is to be *kept* by us, not *created* by us. Armed with the right attitude, assigned the right task, what we now need is the right foundation. What foundation does Paul declare as the basis of this unity?

There is already one body because there is one Spirit. There is one hope of our calling. Only one Lord. Only one faith. Only one baptism. And above, through and in us, there is one God and Father (vv. 4–6). In heaven is the triune God, and on earth we find a common confessed faith and a common baptism—Word and sacrament. It is striking that there are no governmental bonds referred to here; the bonds are of another nature entirely. He does not list one holy father in Rome. Nor does he say one ecumenical headquarters in New York. He does not refer to summit leadership conferences in Colorado

Springs. When Paul is appealing to Christians to maintain the unity they already have, he appeals to them on this basis—one Lord, one faith, one baptism.

Of course, this does not mean that the ministry is irrelevant to this question of unity. In the next breath, Paul goes on to say that the one Lord ascended into heaven, and from that exalted place He gave the gift of godly ministry to men: "And he gave some, apostles; and some, prophets; and some, evangelists; and some, pastors and teachers" (Eph. 4:11). The reason He did this was so that these officers would labor in the perfecting of the saints, building up the body of Christ *until we all come to the unity of the faith* (vv. 12-13). The task before these officers is the presentation of a perfect man, a Church that has grown up into the measure of the fullness of Christ (v. 13).

This means the saints are exhorted to have an attitude of humility and patience as they endeavor to preserve that measure of unity they already have, a unity created by the Spirit of God. At the same time, they clearly do not yet have the *full* measure of the unity that God intends for His Church. Because of the unity we have, we are to strive for the unity we do not have.

In summary, Paul teaches first that we have a unity that must be preserved. He also teaches that we do not yet have full unity, for that is the pastoral and eschatological goal of those faithful officers, given by Christ, who labor in the Church. And the unity we already have is a unity based upon the unity of God, the unity declared in baptism in the triune Name.

Faithful pastors therefore advance the work of true unity. Unfaithful teachers disrupt that unity and so their lying ministries must themselves be disrupted. As unity grows under a faithful ministry, we are no longer children, tossed to and fro by televangelists, or carried about by every contradictory wind of doctrine to blow out of the magisterium. The work of true unity is not advanced by an irenicism that tolerates the "sleight of men" (Eph. 4:4). A shepherd who tolerates wolves is a shepherd who hates his own sheep. A shepherd who loves his sheep is one who fights the wolves. And the wolves in sheep's clothing don't like this, not at all, and so they always raise the great cry—*unity!*

In dealing with this threat, faithful pastors do not declaim from the pulpit about "wolves abstractly considered." They name names, like Hymaneus and Alexander. And that is why it is treachery to the cause of true unity to refuse to point out obvious departures from the faith—regardless of the honored position of the one departing: "If we or an angel from heaven . . ." (Gal. 1:8). If there really were an unbroken magisterium, a united confession going back to the apostles, a unanimous consent of the fathers, no one would be more excited about it than I. But when such authority is claimed, and cannot be established from the Scriptures, and contradicts itself in a thousand ways even when evaluated in accordance with its own principles, a faithful minister can only label it as a deception.

But pastors are to labor to this end of unity by speaking the truth *in love*, in order that the already unified body might become unified. We are growing up into our head, the Lord Jesus Christ. From Him, the whole body is being joined together—and the picture here of being joined and compacted as every joint supplies is an image of being knit together *in the womb* (Eph. 4:15–16). There is an essential unity in an embryo, but there is also a much higher unity toward which the embryo is growing. Many complaints about the "disunity" of the Church are actually complaints about how God knits in the darkness of the womb. We look over His shoulder and have the temerity to criticize what He is doing there. But we must go by what the Word says, and not by what we see.

So as we grow up toward this unity, to extend the metaphor, we necessarily fight false teachers who want to introduce their birth defects into the process. As we love one another in all humility and stand for the truth in love, we advance the cause of unity in truth. God directs how this process will finally culminate. Our task is not to oversee the whole process, but rather to be faithful and obedient in our small portion of it.

We therefore affirm a doctrine of apostolic succession, but this is not a succession of ordinations. That is not the basis of unity. Rather, it is a succession of baptisms, and all that those baptisms represent. One Lord, one faith, one baptism. (There will be more on this in Chapter V: Authority and Apostolic Succession.) But we receive our inheritance from our Christian past, and we perpetuate it as we evangelize nonbelievers and bring up our children in the faith. We do so by means of Word and sacrament, preaching and baptism. This is the unity we have received from God. As we recognize that all covenant members have received this common inheritance, this gives us the foundation from which to work on improving that unity. We are an embryo in the womb. To look for full governmental unity *now* is to look for a kid in the second trimester to grow Aaron's beard, so that the oil can run down it, to use a grotesque image.

Although I don't have time to argue for this fully here, this is why the postmillennial vision is so important. Postmillennialism argues (on exegetical grounds) that the Church will see days of glory in the future far surpassing anything we have seen up to this point. Postmillennialism argues that the *Church is in fact still an embryo*, and that we will one day be a perfect man.[2] We are not yet that perfect man. Assuming that this is God's decree and that someday this *will* come to pass, then I am obligated as a faithful servant to work and labor in the direction of that decree. I want to show why this is so important for classical Protestants. Without it, there is no way to keep Protestant churches from disintegrating into a sect mentality. If God has no plan for the Church in history, then *we* need not have one. If there is no *telos* toward which we are growing, then we need not have any regard for it. In another variation of this, if the "perfect man" that the Bible talks about is manifest only in heaven, then there is no pressing need to strive toward that perfect man on

---

[2] It needs to be said here that I understand that many solid Protestants are not postmill like I am, and so this line of argument will not seem as compelling to them. And I should also acknowledge that John Henry Newman appeals to the "embryonic" argument also, and so a separate discussion has to be developed there. In the meantime, before the church grows into a full eschatological glory, all Protestants have a different understanding of what constitutes true unity, an understanding that encompasses all of church history.

earth. (See my book *Heaven Misplaced* for a further discussion of this.)

Consequently, in my view, the error of Protestant sects is that of assuming that God has no earthly plan for the history of the institutional Church and that there is no embryo at all. What you see around you is what God wanted from the beginning, which is to say, a fragmented, scattered collection of churches. All things will be put right in heaven, they affirm, but in the meantime the earthly pandemonium is actually a design feature.

But the contrary error of Rome is that of assuming the embryo is already fully grown in all essential respects. But this leads to an *a priori* inability to see a new historic work of the Spirit. The historic Protestant looks at the current problems and affirms that God is sovereign over all such apparent impediments. The sin *will* be dealt with, and some things that looked like a bad business to us will actually be revealed as having a larger divine purpose. When God wants to knit a perfect man throughout the course of a sinful, fallen world, He does so. The fact that He knows what He is doing should be apparent to us by now. But we continue to write Him off, as though His prophecies on this subject will somehow fall to the ground.

This means that I believe in the eventual reunion of all covenantal communions. This extends even to the Jews, as Paul notes in Romans 11. If wild olive branches could be grafted into the cultivated tree and yet grow, what will happen when the natural branches are grafted back in? Life from the dead. The only communions that will not be grafted back into the one olive tree will be those communions that no longer exist. The church in Ephesus had her lampstand removed, and the church is no longer there at all. No one is there except for the tourists among the ruins.

Paul expressly warned the church at Rome that she was vulnerable to the same judgment that befell the Jews, and that she had to guard against the hubris that set the Jews up for their fall. I do not believe they heeded the warning, just as the Jews did not. But this does not slow God down any—let God be true and every man a liar. If Rome was cut out, she can be grafted back in. If Rome was not cut out, but only radically cut *back*, she will flourish and bear evangelical fruit once again.

So this is what I mean by eventual reunion: one Lord, one faith, one baptism, one church.

CHAPTER II

Love the One You're With

I was once in a conversation with a group of friends, and the subject of the Scottish covenanters came up. I forget exactly how we got there, but one friend was not sure how much actual sympathy he had for the covenanters, thinking that there was more than a little fanaticism in their stand. Courage and martyrdom are all very well, but would it have hurt anyone to take a more moderate and sane stand in the face of persecution? My response to him lies at the heart of my thoughts here. I want to address obedience and the affections. Another way to speak of this is in terms of covenant loyalty.

I think his comment was misplaced precisely because he was in large measure right. In other words, covenant loyalty understands the concept of social and corporate justification. (Individual justification by imputation is the subject of Chapter XII.) I am quite prepared to believe that many die-hard Protestants down through the years have been fanatical, unwieldy, and hard to deal with. Sometimes this was due to their righteousness, the kind of person of whom the world was not worthy. You probably would not invite the Tishbite to a wine and cheese *soiree*, or Jenny Geddes either, for that matter. Sometimes it was due to them being right in a wrong kind of way. But such angularities do not keep them from being *my* people. Having a crazy uncle in the attic does not undo the bloodlines—he is still my uncle. Sometimes I support my uncle, sometimes oppose him, but he is always my uncle.

I mentioned in my discussion with my friend that the same principle applied to our understanding of the early church. In the many waves of persecution that swept over the Church, one effect of this was that moderate and tempered responses were not elicited from the ranks of the faithful. Origen's mother had to hide Origen's clothes so that he would not run outside to get himself arrested in order to be martyred. In the frenzy of pagan persecution, did all early Christians behave as though they were being invited to a game of lawn tennis? Not a bit of it. Consequently, in the early history of the Church there were many fanatics—but they are my people nonetheless.

The same could be said of asceticism, particularly the Syrian strain of it. For example, people sat on the top of poles for decades to avoid worldliness. Men and women would live together in celibate marriage, which caused consternation at different church councils like Elvira and Nicea. John Chrysostom, during his monkish stay up in the mountains, did not lie down, ever, for two years. He slept standing up, a fairly common practice among the monks. What good did *that* do? Well, during that time Chrysostom memorized the Old and New Testaments. In short, the first four centuries of the Church are filled with some glorious weirdos. In fact, one of the charges brought against John Chrysostom at the Synod of the Oaks was that he had called Epiphanius a babbler and a little weirdo.

Now, all these people, being Christian, are in the covenant together with me, over against the Hindus, say. Because of this, I have to "answer" for them in some sense. Because of the covenant link, I have obligations. Those obligations range from full support to manic opposition, depending on the circumstances. But whether I support or oppose them, our shared baptisms in the triune name mean that we have a shared identity. Triune baptism is never false—let God be true and every man a liar. An unsympathetic observer would say that I am "making excuses" for people I agree with, and that I am inconsistently hard on those I disagree with. No, I am simply saying that "identity with" or "lack of identity with" is the necessary context for all forms of support or opposition. I have a shared human identity with a Hindu (*imago Dei*) which would become obvious, for example, if we were working together to get people out of a burning building. I have a shared Christian identity with anyone baptized in the name of the triune God, which would be obvious over against Muslim terrorists. But other complicating factors can get thrown into the mix, like national and cultural identities, which sometimes are promoted to a level they should not enjoy. An American atheist and an American Christian might have an easier time of it sharing a meal in a restaurant than the American Christian would with a Bantu Christian.

Now every such group "justifies" those inside, and refuses "justification" to those outside. I am not here speaking of justification in the theological sense as it applies to individuals. I am speaking of the impulse that makes us say, silently, "Yes, my sister is ugly, but *you* can't say that." In other words, "you" are outside the group or family and have no standing to bring a charge. The charge may be true, but "you" still do not have standing. This impulse to social justification is apparent everywhere—in racial hatreds, in nationalist collisions, and in religious disputes such as the one we are examining. Those in the "justified" group are judicially innocent, though they may be acknowledged as personally guilty. This is why we hear things like, "Yes, so and so did thus and such, *but* . . ." The *yes* acknowledges the personal guilt and the *but* leads into some acknowledgment of his social position among "the justified." Thus, a green activist will say, "Yes, shooting loggers is a bit extreme, but we have to remember our forests are being decimated." The activist may genuinely be appalled at what his fellow green did, but that identity is still there, and he must function within the boundaries of this social justification—because the only alternative is going over to the other side. When this justification mechanism is operating on all cylinders, it can swallow the most horrendous and indefensible activities—which is what I see in the case of the suicide bombers in Israel. A bomber could kill everyone at a six-year-old's birthday party, and the explanation would still follow. "Our group disavows this action, *but* . . ."

As sinful as some forms of this craven excuse-making are, other forms of justification are inescapable. This is because it is impossible to opt out of the system entirely. As we discuss the issues surrounding the Reformation, nobody comes at it as a disinterested party or "objective" historian: We justify according to the side that has our affections. I hope I have not muddied up a relatively simple point.

Say I were having a discussion with a Protestant on the threshold of conversion to Catholicism. (Now for the record, the issue between such a person and me is not the same as it would be if I, raised Protestant, were discussing this with someone raised Catholic.) In such a situation, he and I are members of the same denomination and come under the same authority. He has come to a threshold of conversion, which means that his affections have moved elsewhere. (I am using "affection" in this sense of the social justification that I am describing, not in the sense of personal affection for particular individuals.)

This is why he and I could compare the following sentences and see striking similarities.

"Yes, I agree that the Catholic church has been wracked with sexual scandal, but . . ."

"Yes, I agree that Protestant churches are shot through with individualism, but. . ."

If we climb into our respective propositions, we could play paradigm bumper cars all day long and not get anywhere. This is why I would want all this to lead up to an appeal to his remaining Protestant affections, which, because he is not a machine made out of stainless steel, I know are still there.

Because his affections have significantly moved, I believe that he is vulnerable to the temptation to justify what he is moving to in the sense I have already described above. Because his affections have moved, he justifies certain things, and has come to love a certain *idea*.

But I want to bring this idea down to earth with a thud. Over the course of my life I have spent a lot of time around Roman Catholics—my dearest friend in the Navy was the Catholic lay leader. (I was the Protestant lay leader.) I do not believe my judgments are those of an uninformed bigot. I have certainly been around Roman Catholics long enough to have a sense of their spiritual pulse, generally speaking. Doctrine aside, I am speaking of incarnational living—the level of Marian obedience. Given this incarnational reality, if he continues to pursue the course he is on, who will his children marry? What will the character of *their* faith be like twenty years from now? Will his grandchildren love and serve the Lord Jesus Christ with heart, soul, mind and strength? Will they grow up in the faith in a way that goes beyond a mere assent to certain propositions? Will they love God in daily practical ways? I hope so, and I even think it possible. But if I were to measure by my experience, to embrace that possibility as a *likelihood* would be the triumph of hope over experience. Such a person may feel this to be an unfair *ad hominem*, but I do not intend this in an insulting way at all.

Bishop Sheen once sent a manuscript to the printers, and when the galleys came back to him, he noted that *Heaven* and *Hell* were all reduced to the lower case, *heaven* and *hell*. He dutifully corrected them, and sent it back. He got into a tussle with his editor over this, and his editor asked him why he wanted them in the upper case. "Because," said the bishop, "they are *places*. You know, like Scarsdale." I would ask such a man, as one who must give an account for his soul, and the souls of those in his household, "Where are you taking them? Where are you taking your grandchildren and great-grandchildren?"

CHAPTER III

The Ultimate Letter to Rome

Once we get past our agreement that perseverance in the faith should be considered a good thing, the doctrine of perseverance creates a large number of questions. Some of the disagreements that arise out of this are extremely subtle, so it is important to define our terms very carefully at the outset.

According to the historic Reformed faith, the elect of God cannot fall away. This is not because they are made out of stainless steel—they are as frail as the non-elect and can in fact be broken. But the Word of God cannot be broken. If God has spoken a persevering word concerning them in His secret counsels, then that word cannot be broken. Believers are bone of Christ's bones and flesh of His flesh. The Word tells us that Christ's physical bones could not be broken (Jn. 19:36), but this did not mean that his bones were made out of a material different from ours. Rather, it meant that God would providentially preserve His bones from being broken. Christ's bones were breakable just like ours, but God's Word is not breakable. In a similar way, we are His bones and so the elect will persevere. In *themselves*, the elect are capable of falling away, but in the decrees of God they are completely secure. The elect will in fact persevere. In an ultimate sense, this is tautological because in the Reformed faith those who are elect are defined as those who do in fact persevere.

But it is not the case that all covenant members persevere. The New Testament is filled with warnings about falling away, and their contexts reveal that these warnings are not hypothetical. Branches in Christ are cut off and taken away for their fruitlessness (Jn. 15:1–6) and the Jewish branches of the olive tree *were* removed (Rom. 11:20). There is such a thing as union with Christ from which apostasy is possible. The difference between those who are kept by God's persevering grace and those who are not is a very real difference, but it is a difference known only to God (Deut. 29:29). Nevertheless, it is a central theme in classical Protestant thinking that the elect will of necessity persevere.

In contrast to this, Rome teaches that mortal sin can be committed by anyone, from the highest to the lowest, and if they die without receiving forgiveness for such mortal sin, then they are condemned regardless of who they are. This is why Dante, a devout Catholic, had no trouble populating his inferno with various ecclesiastical dignitaries. This is sometimes surprising to modern Protestants, who see this as a protest of some sort against the medieval Church. It is protest, certainly, but a protest against moral corruption and disorder, not a protest against Catholic teaching *per se*. (It is completely faithful to that teaching.) We have trouble with this because of our modernist sectarian mindset. If an alumnus of Liberty University wrote a novel in which Jerry Falwell was relegated to the fifth circle, we would all take this as a protest against the entire "sect." But the Roman Catholic position is that their whole is far greater than the sum of its parts. Ten popes in a row, and twenty platoons of cardinals, could all die and go to Hell, but nevertheless the Church would not and could not fail. And further, this would not refute the Church; it is the doctrine *of* the Church.

And this is why Rome has a doctrine of perseverance. This guaranteed perseverance is assured to the Church at Rome, but not necessarily to any individuals within it. The historic Reformed faith reverses this—any particular church can have its lamp stand removed, but the elect cannot fall away. Rome and Geneva agree that the "catholic church" cannot fall away, but differ on what constitutes that "catholic church."

In other words, it is a matter of faith for Roman Catholics that the Church at Rome as an institution cannot be guilty of apostasy. The lampstand at Ephesus could be removed (Rev. 2:5), and, as historical events have shown, was removed: There is nothing at Ephesus now but rubble and tourists with cameras. But to take this imagery from Asia Minor westward, according to the magisterium of Rome, the lampstand of Rome cannot be removed. The constancy of Rome is a given. With regard to apostasy, Rome is indefectible. As the Catechism of the Catholic Church puts it, "The Church . . . is held, as a matter of faith, to be unfailingly holy" (823)[3]. This

---

[3] "Catechism of the Catholic Church," The Holy See, 823, http://www.vatican.va/archive/ENG0015/_INDExod.HTM [accessed 9/26/2015].

is not a claim of perfection (825), but it is a claim that apostasy cannot happen to the Roman Church.

In the debates between Roman Catholics and us "Protesting Catholics" (or "Reformed Catholics," if you will), this issue is one of foundational importance. It operates as an axiomatic presupposition and is often the reason why other lesser debates get nowhere. If there is a foundational assumption that Rome cannot fall away into damnable error, it is useless to try to show how Rome has taught some damnable error or another—say, on Mary, indulgences, or whatnot. For the Protesting Catholic, since he has the assumption that the particular church at Rome *could* fall away into such error, it is a simple matter of examining this or that issue to see if it is an example of that kind of error. The question can be answered.

This is a root issue, therefore, and debating it is important. At the same time, it is a debate at the presuppositional level and cannot be treated as though it were a detail. This indefectibility of Rome is the *sine qua non* of the Roman Catholic system. If it is not true, then everything else falls with it. If it is true, then the system as a whole stands. If the axe is to be laid at the root of the tree, this would be the trunk.

It is not observed frequently enough that the reason for this is partly the fault of our modern individualism, which treats the Bible as the Book that Fell from the Sky, for the sole purpose of providing all of us with raw material for our Quiet Times. In this, we have rushed ahead to application, and have neglected one of the first rules of clear-headed Bible reading. The Bible is a collection of documents for the *Church*; it is the library of the Church—the first and foundational church library. We can say that it is, in a certain limited sense, *for* every individual Christian, but we cannot say that it was written *to* every individual Christian. And in order for us to find out what it means for us, we have to first determine what it meant for the people who received it at the first. The order is this: the Word of God comes, first, *to* those to whom it is addressed, second, it is *for* the entire Church of God, and third, in descending order of importance, we may say that it is *for* the individual Christian.

When Jeremiah was told he would not marry or have sons or daughters in that place (Jer. 16:1–2), this was written to Jeremiah while living in the land of Israel right before the Babylonian exile. But if I assume it was written to me, I might make some bad decisions with long term consequences. It is *for* me, but not *to* me. The Scriptures are for the entire Church, but the entire Church has to take into account the name that was on the first envelope.

This has a striking application when we consider the letter to the Church at Rome. We who are "Reformed Catholics" are in a contest with the Church at Rome. But unlike our contests with various heresies, sects and cults—the kind plentiful in our day, the kind that probably started in Kansas City fifty years ago—we are in a contest with a church actually mentioned in the Bible. The book of Romans is a letter in the Bible addressed to that church. One of St. Paul's friends, a man named Clement, became the functional bishop of that Church. Now, if one of the New Testament epistles had been written to Tenth Pres in Philadelphia, it would be illegitimate for that particular church to let that letter become part of a generic Bible, blending into the background. They would be required to remember what had been said *to them*. So in a very real way, the book of Romans is a covenant possession of the Church of Rome and belongs in the Vatican library. Also, in a real way, that letter stands as a Song of Moses to them; it is a testimony against them. In multiple ways, the Church of Rome formally denies various doctrines which *their* letter requires them to affirm.

Paul says this: "To *all that be in Rome*, beloved of God, called to be saints: Grace to you and peace from God our Father, and the Lord Jesus Christ" (Rom. 1:7). A few verses down, he says, "So, as much as in me is, I am ready to preach the gospel *to you that are at Rome* also" (Rom. 1:15). And in writing to the Romans, St. Paul addresses one issue that involves more than the immediate present. He contrasts the exclusion of the Jews to the inclusion of the Gentiles and tells the Gentiles not to become haughty about this. They are warned against the sin committed by the Jews, who had become guilty of a covenantal presumption: "*We* are the sons of Abraham." This temptation had the force it did precisely because of the long and ancient tradition the Jews had inherited from the time of Abraham. The biblical answer to this sin was that God could make sons of Abraham out of rocks.

Now Abraham had received the promises almost two thousand years before his descendants were removed from the covenant. Such a long period presents quite a bit of time in which covenantal arrogance can build up. Now Paul warns the Romans against *falling into this same sin*. The warning was necessary at the time—in other words, Paul saw reasons in the first century to give the warning.

Rome was the capital city of a great empire, and one of the most natural temptations would be to think that the church in such a city had preeminence over the community church in East Toad Flats, Arkansas. Furthermore, given the nature of the sin, *the warning becomes increasingly pertinent over time*. However, regardless of the reasons for issuing the warning, Paul is explicit in the nature of his warning. It is worth quoting at length, and the emphases are obviously mine.

> For I speak to you Gentiles, inasmuch as I am the apostle of the Gentiles, I magnify mine office: If by any means I may provoke to emulation them which are my flesh, and might save some of them. For if the casting away of them be the reconciling of the world, what shall the receiving of them be, but life from the dead? For if the firstfruit be holy, the lump is also holy: and if the root be holy, so are the branches. And if some of the branches be broken off, and thou, being a wild olive tree, wert graffed in among them, and with them partakest of the root and fatness of the olive tree; Boast not against the branches. But *if thou boast, thou bearest not the root, but the root thee.* Thou wilt say then, The branches were broken off, that I might be graffed in. Well; *because of unbelief they were broken off, and thou standest by faith. Be not highminded, but*

fear: For if God spared not the natural branches, *take heed lest he also spare not thee*. Behold therefore the goodness and severity of God: on them which fell, severity; but toward thee, goodness, if thou continue in his goodness: *otherwise thou also shalt be cut off.* (Rom. 11:13–22)

The apostle to the Gentiles wrote a letter to the preeminent church of the Gentile world. In this letter, he tells them not to boast over against the Jews who were removed. He reminds the Church at Rome that they are *not* the root, and that they do *not* bear the root. Rather the root bears them and is distinct from them. The Jews were cut off because of unbelief, and the only reason that the Church of Rome was in the olive tree at all was because of faith—they stood by faith. He tells them to avoid high-mindedness, and instead of this high-mindedness, they were to fear. If God was willing to cut out the Jews, why would He refuse to cut out Johnny-come-lately Roman Gentiles? Why would he refuse to cut out the particular Church of the Gentiles that he was addressing when Paul wrote this? *That particular* church was commanded to "take heed" concerning this issue. The Church of Rome was commanded to continue in God's goodness to them, and they were told that if they did not, they would also be cut off, just like the Jews had been.

The warnings were heeded—for a time. Centuries later, Gregory the Great rejected the title of universal bishop in his famous controversy with the patriarch of Constantinople precisely because of the sin against humility it represented. To assume such a title, Gregory thought, was to be antichrist. It is important to note that Gregory was not fighting for the right to use the title himself. When the bishop of Alexandria referred to Gregory as "Universal Pope," Gregory refused the title. He claimed that it would puff up vanity and damage Christian charity, which, when his example was later neglected, it most certainly did. Obedience to Paul's charge is part of the background here.

Clement of Rome, a friend of Paul's, and a man who served as the functional bishop of Rome from 92 to 101, provides an earlier example of one who heard and *heeded* Paul's warning against this kind of hubris. He was certainly no egalitarian—his letter to the Corinthians rebuked them for the rebellion against their elders. That was the point of his letter. He said, "The great cannot exist without the small; neither can the small exist without the great: there is a certain mutuality in the whole, and this is beneficial to it" (37:4). Like Paul, he had no problem with authority, whether scriptural or ecclesiastical. Jesus teaches us that men should *want* to be great in the kingdom of heaven, and such greatness would certainly involve spiritual authority. But Jesus also tells us *how* this is to be done—and not done:

> But Jesus called them unto him, and said, Ye know that the princes of the Gentiles exercise dominion over them, and they that are great exercise authority upon them. But it shall not be so among you: but whosoever will be great among you, let him be your minister; And whosoever will be chief among you, let him be your servant: Even as the Son of man came not to be ministered unto, but to minister, and to give his life a ransom for many. (Mt. 20:25–28)

And this is why Clement had a problem with ecclesiastical arrogance: "For it is to the humble that Christ belongs, not to those who exalt themselves over his flock. The scepter of the majesty of God, the Lord Jesus Christ, did not come with the pomp of pride or arrogance, though he could have, but in humility" (16:1–2). Clement of Rome served the Church at Rome from 92 to 101. He was an admirable bishop in every respect, and the miter he wore was one of humility.

SECTION TWO

HARMONY

CHAPTER IV

A Work of High Harmony

I once received a question from an old acquaintance, keying off a discussion of Eastern Orthodoxy that I had had. Here is the question:

> On what grounds do you reject the authority of the 7th Ecumenical Council? As Christians, we consider the JW's (for example) outside the church, because they reject the teachings of other councils. They do so because they believe these teachings are contrary to Scripture. It seems the question is, "who decides what defines Christianity?"

Let me set aside the "Jehovah's Witnesses" part quickly. We have to make a distinction between the formal ground of appeal and whether or not such an appeal is sustained by the document appealed to. The fact that the JWs *say* that they care about Scripture more than subsequent creeds is fine. But it is *not* fine for them to say that, and then go on to twist the Scriptures out of all recognition (2 Pet. 3:16). If they appeal to Scriptures, to the Scriptures let us go. And they shall suddenly be confounded and discover that they have another appointment they need to get to. We are not sure who it is with, but it is probably with someone who doesn't know the Bible.

But behind this initial distraction, I think the central question posed is an important question, and there are three things I would want to note about it. Keep in mind that this is just the outline of my position—much more could be developed within this framework. Someday, after I am an archbishop and past grace, I will no doubt have the time to devote to it.

First, to set the stage (and *not* to poison the well, despite appearances) I would want to note that in Scripture, "whose authority…" is the devil's question. When Jesus came to Israel, He did not fit with the expectations of the official religious handlers—a kind of person who has not gone away since that time, incidentally. They came to Him with what seemed to them the most obvious question in the world, which amounted to "where do *you* get off? Papers, please."

"And when he was come into the temple, the chief priests and the elders of the people came unto him as he was teaching, and said, By what authority doest thou these things? and who gave thee this authority?" (Mt. 21:23; cf. Mk. 11:28; Lk. 20:2).

This observation doesn't settle anything by itself, but it should make us go *hmmmm*.

But second, just because it is the devil's question doesn't mean that we shouldn't answer it—but it does mean that we need to be careful when we do. So, I reject the authority of the Church as expressed in the Seventh Ecumenical Council because I accept the authority of the Church as expressed in the Bible's Table of Contents. The Table of Contents found at the beginning of every edition of the Scriptures I have ever seen is the foundational Creed of the Church. It is no more inspired than the maps and concordance are, but it is much more authoritative. It outranks, by definition, every other creed.

I submit to the determination of the Church that "this" is the canon of Scripture, and I submit also to what follows from that. Scripture is full of revealed content, received by us as the intelligible Word of God. This is the universal testimony of the Church—Scripture is God speaking. As revealed content, the Bible was not meant to be put under glass in a museum. It was written so that we might read and understand it, and then act upon it. And one of the scenarios we find repeatedly within Scripture—the Scripture testified to by the Church, remember—is the phenomenon of officers to the Word trying to seize mastery and control over the Word. That is an important (and very clear) theme throughout the Scriptures.

Now these are the Scriptures that the universal Church has told me are the very words of God. The universal Church has *not* told me the same thing about her own words. There are Bibles in churches, but there are also churches in the Bible. The second narrative is normative and informs our understanding of the first one.

The Bible tells me that the Church is my mother (Gal. 4:26), and that I am to honor her (Exod. 20:12). But the Scriptures also tell me that I am not to follow what she says if she has been hitting the gin cabinet again (Acts 7:51), which in certain ages she has sometimes done.

Now many Protestants (in my opinion) do make a category mistake in their debates with Roman Catholics and the Orthodox on this point. On a practical level I have no problem answering a false tradition of men with Scripture, as Jesus did (Mt. 15:3), and as I did with my first point. The problem of a category mistake arises later, if we are working through the matter on the epistemological level. There the question should be Creed against Creed, Council against Council, and not (in the first instance) Council against Scripture.

Because the Bible is the Word of God, we do not have to arrange our systematic theologies according to the verses that are entirely true, those that are mostly true, those that are partly true, and so forth. The Scriptures are the Word of God, refined seven-fold (Ps. 12:6). This is not true of creeds and councils. Everybody looking at church history has to pick which ones they will go with and which ones they will snort at as self-evidently spurious. When I do what I do, I believe it is fair for someone to ask me "by what standard?" My approach is dictated by my acceptance of the Church's testimony of the canon of Scripture, and by the fact that somebody taught me to read.

Let me give one of many examples. Having been pointed to the Bible by the Church (godly parents, the *ministerium* of the church, and many sword drills in Southern Baptist Sunday School), I have gone on to read that I must not worship images (Exod. 20:4; cf. Council of Hieria, 754 A.D.). You say that Second Nicea (787) repudiated Hieria? Shoot! Who can tell anymore? I give up. Back to Exodus 20.

But thus exasperated, I do not retreat to a Bible as the Book that Fell From the Sky. I do receive it from the Church, and I accept the foundational creed of the Church, the Table of Contents. I accept, as a corollary, all that is contained in those books. To get anywhere with me on this point, you would have to persuade me that the universal Church has not testified that the Scriptures are the Word of God. And if they are, then let's have a Bible study. So just as John the Baptist pointed to Jesus without outranking Him, so also the Church pointed to the Scriptures in the Canon without outranking the Canon.

My third and last point concerns the role of the Holy Spirit in all of this. My decision-making about "who has the authority" to speak to me about the condition of my soul revolves around the work of the

Holy Spirit. Jesus is the way to the Father (Jn. 14:6), and He also describes Himself there as the *truth* and the *life*. Since He has ascended into Heaven, the way, the truth, and the life are found through the Holy Spirit. The "tells" of His presence are described fully in the Scriptures, so that we would make no mistake concerning it. He manifests His presence through love, joy, peace, patience, kindness, goodness, faithfulness, gentleness, and self-control. None of this is possible without full and free forgiveness, and this is not possible without a blood-true gospel.

So as I seek out a people to worship with, I am interested in the maximum amount of truth and the fullest expression of life. *These two together in high harmony* are the work of the Spirit, and it is a work that only He can do. Without Him, we separate them, and either veer off into a view of truth that treats doctrines like so many beetles pinned to corkboards, or into life as an anarchistic laugh riot. In the end we lose the very thing we detached from the other in order to pursue it in a self-serving way.

With Cyprian, I believe that where the Spirit is, there is the Church. When we are told that Jesus taught with authority, and not like the scribes (Mt. 7:29), we were learning about the work of the Spirit. We are not being told that Jesus had His diploma with Him and the rabbis didn't. Where the Spirit is, there is true authority. And it is always more than sufficient.

CHAPTER V

Authority and Apostolic Succession

A number of years ago I had a number of friends who maintained that the way to argue with me was to answer *yes* to the first question I asked (whatever it was), and then to stoutly say *no* thereafter. I mention this because I am about to attempt something that I think our Roman Catholic friends might want to respond to in this way.

Let's begin with some debris clearing. There are just a few random items that should be set out publicly at the front end of this discussion. And after doing so, I want to present an argument for a form of apostolic succession that is consistent with the tenets of classical Protestantism, and not consistent with apostolic succession as held by Rome and Eastern Orthodoxy (and some Anglicans).

First, to argue for the necessity of apostolic succession (as I want to do) is not to treat apostolic succession as operating like some kind of simple electrical current, where if the circuit is broken at any one place you have no power on the other end. It is more like a vast continent-wide grid (if you want to use electricity as an example), or to use St. Peter's illustration (and that of many other biblical writers) it is like water flooding the world, as it did in the days of Noah. This is a figure, Peter says, of *baptism*, about which we will visit later.

Second, while we happily acknowledge that apostolic succession is an important question, and it is related to the question of authority, which is really *the* fundamental question, we have to acknowledge (and I would press my friends in Rome to acknowledge it) that there is a way of asking the authority question that puts you in dubious company. If the kingdom of God were like a pure line of Labrador retrievers, where we always had to have our pedigree papers stamped by the authorities in Jerusalem, then certain notables of our faith would be in trouble. I speak, of course, about John the Baptist. Tell me, was he authorized or not? Was he from heaven, or not? And the question was posed to Jesus as well. "And when he was come into the temple, the chief priests and the elders of the people came unto him as he was teaching, and said, *By what authority* doest thou these things? and who gave thee this authority? (Mt. 21:23). Asked in a certain way, this is the devil's question. Now I cheerfully acknowledge that there is a good and God-honoring way to ask the question. It just needs to be noted that it is not *automatically* a good question. Throughout the long history of the covenant people, God has always loved to send disreputable messengers out of the wilderness into the royal and priestly courts and, once there, to have them behave in uncertified ways.

Third, when it comes to issues of "where are we to find the visible church," there are two basic ways to address the question. The first is to argue for some form of succession and the second is to argue for some form of restoration. The former option is taken by Roman Catholics, Eastern Orthodox, and classical Protestants. Surprisingly to some, this is also the historic Baptist position. The differences are found in how succession is to be recognized, measured and noted, and not whether it is occurring. The restorationist position is found with groups like the Church of Christ, or out on the cultic edge, the LDS movement. The idea here is that the true church of Jesus Christ fell off the planet at some point after the apostles died, and then had to be restored, in effect from scratch.

This helps explain how classical Protestants can identify with the Church as she existed prior to the Reformation. In answer to the question, "Where was your Church before the Reformation?" the answer is, "Where was your face before you washed it?" The Reformation was a reformation of a portion of an existing Church, not the formation of a new church or denomination. I want to argue that such an identification with the ancient and medieval church is necessary if we are to avoid a cultic or sectarian mentality. But in order to be able to do this, we need a doctrine of apostolic succession, one that is biblically-grounded in the first place, and deals with the historical data (so far as it exists) in the second place.

This brings us to another detail that needs to be addressed before we get into the argument. All of us bring certain faith assumptions to our examination of church history. These faith assumptions do two things: they are the grid through which we interpret existing data, and they are the grid by which we fill in the gaps. I confess that I do not have notarized minutes from elder meetings going all the way back. *Nobody* does. Even when a claim is made that a particular communion has a line of bishops all the way back, certain gaps still have to be filled in. For example, was Clement of Rome a pope? As one Jesuit writer, Francis Sullivan, demonstrates in his book *From Apostles to Bishops*, we do not have historical grounds for saying that Clement was a bishop at all, still less a universal bishop. Sullivan, of course, believes that he was, but he also knows that it cannot be shown from the records of the early fathers. Every position involved in this discussion has to deal with notable gaps, which in my mind is not an argument against any of them. We all fill in these gaps by faith, established on other grounds. My point is simply that these gaps cannot be used against the Protestants only. In fact, the demonstrable existence of such gaps favors a position that allows for them (like classical Protestantism) and argues against any position that depends on an absence of gaps. In this sense, the history of the early church is a very great friend of the classical Protestant position.

All this said, I want to note that the foundation for my faith assumptions about church history are found in Scripture. This means that I believe certain things about the authority of the Church on the basis of what Jesus and the apostles taught, not because I can produce an exhaustive set of minutes that prove, say, that Second Nicea was an unlawful council. I know what to think of Second Nicea on the basis of the Second Commandment, which I consider to be a senior "Second."

One last thing before we begin. Questions of scriptural authority cannot be separated from questions of ecclesiastical authority. The Bible, all 66 books of it, is the Word of God and is the final and ultimate authority over all our disputes. But we have to acknowledge the role that Church played in the formation of that canon. The Table of Contents in front of my Bible is not the Word of God directly, but is rather the work of the Holy Spirit in and through the Church. The Bible is not the Book that Fell from the Sky. This ecclesiastical authority is not over Scripture, any more than John's testimony that Jesus was the "Lamb of God that takes away the sin of the world" places John the Baptist in authority over Christ. That would be obviously absurd, but some Protestants need to learn how to receive John's testimony rightly. The Church is not over Scripture, but the Church points faithfully to Scripture. And in the spirit of John the Baptist, the faithful Church says that Scripture must increase, and I must decrease.

Okay, so now we are ready to start. For those who want to do some background spadework on this question, I am depending on Peter Leithart's wonderful article, "The Womb of the World."[4] Peter is not responsible for the conclusion I am arguing for here, but he is certainly responsible for first pointing me to the premises.

So here is the argument. Hebrews 10:19–22 says this: "Having therefore, brethren, boldness to enter into the holiest by the blood of Jesus, by a new and living way, which he hath consecrated for us, through the veil, that is to say, his flesh; and having an high priest over the house of God; let us draw near with a true heart in full assurance of faith, having our hearts sprinkled from an evil conscience, and our bodies washed with pure water."

The question to which most of us can answer *yes* is this one: may we agree that this is a baptismal text? When we are encouraged by the fact that our bodies are "washed with pure water," are we not being encouraged by the fact that we are baptized into the triune name? Most exegetes do hold this to be a

---

4 Peter Leithart, "The Womb of the World," *Journal of the Study of the New Testament* 22, no. 78 (October 2000): 49–65.

baptismal text, and this appears to make good sense of the passage and context. But then here is the kicker: Just as the Lord's Supper is a rite that fulfills, not only Passover, but all the feasts and sacrifices of Old Israel, so baptism fulfills, not only circumcision, but also a number of other typological features of life under the law, *including the rite of ordination*.

We see this in our text. Our hearts have been *sprinkled* from an evil conscience. What allusion is being made here, especially given the combination of blood and water? Leithart points out that to "draw near, one must come under blood and water—a comparatively rare combination in Levitical law but found in the ordination rite (Exod. 29:4, 21; Lev. 8:6, 30). Hebrews 10:22 describes baptism with imagery borrowed from ordination."[5] And later, Leithart says, "All those baptized and sprinkled with the blood of Christ have privileges of access beyond those of Israel's High Priests."[6]

We Christians in the New Israel are a nation of priests, and as priests, we have access to the heavenly sanctuary. This privilege is conferred, stated, promised, signed, and sealed in our baptisms. Apostolic succession is therefore a priestly

---

5 Leithart, 54.
6 Ibid., 55.

succession, and the New Testament teaches that even Gentiles (in Christ) can walk into the Holy of Holies as priests. Not just one Jew from the line of Aaron, once a year, but multitudes of Gentiles, all the time, not to mention all the Jews who came to faith as well. This means that ordination in the Old Covenant is not primarily a type of ordinations in the New (although there are ordinations in the New). These ancient ordinations are a type of what is declared of all Christians in baptism.

Put another way, although I am an ordained minister, I do not believe that I am at the tail end of a long chain of governmental ordinations going back to Christ. But this does *not* mean that I do not believe in apostolic succession. I am also baptized, and I *do* believe there is a web of baptisms that go all the way back. Christian baptism is *the inundation of the world* and, like the water flowing out over the threshold of Ezekiel's Temple, it only gets deeper and deeper as it goes. The farther we get away from the apostolic era, the wetter the world gets. If we see apostolic succession in terms of mere governmental actions, carefully noted in the minutes, the farther we get away from the apostles, the more obscurity will surround the entire question, and the disputes will multiply. I mean, look at them. Look at *us*.

If in order to offer the bread of life and the wine of the new covenant to our people I have to be sure of the exact relationship between Clement and Linus and other early pastors in Rome, the people of God will starve to death. If, before I open the Scriptures to declare what God has given to all of us, I have to make sure that the electrical current can make it all the way to me through one solitary line, then we are all in trouble.

But it is not this way at all. Jesus never gives us any image of the growth of His kingdom throughout the world that would ever make us think of the phrase "nice and tidy." The kingdom of God is like a dragnet that brings in all kinds of fish, beer bottles, and a bicycle tire. The kingdom of God is like yeast that works through the loaf, and yeast does not grow in straight, neat lines. The kingdom of God is like a mustard seed growing to a large plant, and the birds of their air nest in the branches. The messiness of the Christian world is part of the decretal will of God. The tares in the wheatfield are not behaving, but of course, they never do. The divine will does not color inside the lines that mere men set out for Him. Jesus did pray that His people would be one, as He and the Father are one. This has not happened yet, not *anywhere*. Not in Rome, not in Geneva, not in Constantinople. But Jesus prayed for it, and it will happen. He prayed that the earth would be as full of the Lord as the waters covered the sea. He prayed that He would inherit the ends of the earth for His possession, and He will. The day is coming when the waters of baptism will soak the world. The day is coming when certain Christian communions, bobbing around in their own little boat, will stop claiming that the water exists for their boat only.

The New Testament does teach us that government of the congregation is important, and we see in multiple ways how and why it is important. But John Murray argues rightly that any congregation of baptized Christians, that is to say, any congregation of priests, has the authority to establish such government among themselves. It is necessary that they do so, and the authority conferred by baptism enables them to do so with a clean conscience.

This next thing may seem like an odd claim for a Protestant to make in a discussion with Roman Catholics, but I do not believe that this view is a disparagement of orderly government and ordination on my part, as *their* view is a disparagement of the actual privileges conferred in baptism. Baptism is not just a matter concerning individual salvation, of placing a sign and a seal of Abraham's faith on individual persons. Individuals can be baptized only because the world has been baptized. Baptism is the birthright of the new humanity, the citizenship papers of the inhabitants of the new heaven and new earth. Christ is a new *Adam*. The Church is a new Eve. All things have been made new.

As we congregate in churches, of course all things should be done decently and in order. But our lifeline to Christ is not a line of ordinations, except in the sense that the ordinations of the old order were rolled up into baptism and graciously *given* to us. God has made us kings and priests to rule on the earth. This was conferred upon us when we were baptized into the triune Name, ushered (in that formal rite) into the visible Church.[7]

A position like this makes Christian catholicity, catholicity of spirit, possible. It recognizes the baptisms of all Trinitarian communions, and does not try to solve the lamentable divisions in Christendom by holding up the hands and saying, "Brethren! These divisions are disgraceful! Our proposal for eliminating them is for everyone to stop being obstinate and join us!" At the same time, we all have our own

---

[7] And a special note to my TR friends: I am not denying the reality of heart conversions to God before that point or the absolute covenantal demand for such heart conversion after that point.

views, and nothing whatever can be done about that. But catholicity of spirit requires that we subordinate our views to the profound declaration made in our baptism—one Lord, one faith, one baptism. We subordinate our views, which is not the same thing as abandoning our views. And as this process continues apace, I believe the regrettable errors made by Roman Catholic, Eastern Orthodox, and people just like me do temporarily get in the way of declaring the true unity of that baptism to an unbelieving world.[8]

But we are Christians who believe that God loves the *world*, and we believe that He fully intends to save it. We can therefore afford to be patient. A day is coming when the water will cover the mountain tops.

---

[8] In short, we believe that all the baptized possess collectively and distributively the power that the ministers perform for them as their representatives. What ministers do "in synod" when they formally recognize Scripture is not something beyond the reach of the ordinary Christian.

CHAPTER VI

Personal Judgment

One of the standard charges that is leveled against Protestantism is that *personal judgment* has been a disruptive force in church history, helping to tear the "seamless garment of Christ."

Now obviously, the Protestant Reformation cannot be defended apart from an explanation and defense of what has come to be called "personal judgment." But as with many aspects of Reformed doctrine, this one has to be rescued from the construction that (since the Reformation) has come to be placed upon it. Personal judgment does *not* mean individualistic judgment. Personal judgment, rightly understood is an epistemological question, and not a question of final or ultimate authority.

On the question of authority, classical Protestants and Roman Catholics *agree* that the whims and views of private spirits are not to be considered the ground of any authority whatever. The Christian soul is, by definition, a humble soul in submission. But in submission to what? The classical Protestant answer is that the individual Christian, together with the entire Church, is to be in submission (ultimately) to Scripture. The Roman Catholic answer, in effect, is that the individual Christian is to be in submission to the magisterium of the Church, with no interpretation accepted which is contrary to that magisterium.

In the former, the Church is fallible, and in the latter, the Church is capable of infallibility. In both cases, the individual submits to something outside himself. By way of contrast, the ethos of individualism tends toward the inherent authority of personal judgment.

But reason is an eyeball, and not a source of light. God created us with a faculty for rational weighing and sifting of evidence so that we could submit to light from *outside*. Every form of religion and secularism that tries to make the eyeball shed light is therefore doomed to failure. So Rome and Geneva both agree that the light must come from outside.

But this agreement only goes a limited distance. It would be false to say that submission to external authority eliminates the need for personal judgment. As an epistemological question, personal judgment is an *inescapable* concept. The only question is whether we will exercise it poorly or well, with knowledge or in ignorance. Roman Catholics exercise personal judgment as much as the stoutest Protestant. But for various reasons, they just won't admit what they are doing.

These various reasons include the formal rejection of personal judgment by Rome. For example, the Council of Trent declared, in order to restrain petulant spirits, that no one "relying on his own skill, shall—in matters of faith, and of morals pertaining to the edifications of Christian doctrine—wresting the sacred Scripture to his own senses, presume to interpret the said sacred Scripture contrary to that sense which holy mother Church—whose it is to judge of the true sense and interpretation of the holy Scriptures . . ." (Trent/Session IV).

Vatican I agrees with this, rejecting the heretics that Trent rejected, those heretics who "allowed religious questions to be a matter for the judgment of each individual" (Session III, 5). With this, Vatican II also agrees: "But the task of authentically interpreting the Word of God, whether written or handed on, has been entrusted exclusively to the living teaching office of the Church . . . (*Dei Verbum*, II, 10). Consequently, Roman Catholics who therefore deny that they have the ability to interpret apart from the aid of an infallible interpreter are, in my (private) judgment, understanding the intent of these decrees. But these statements go farther than just saying that private individuals cannot cook up their own truths—the statements have an *epistemological* force. And this leads to problems.

If anyone considers going to Rome, I would want to urge them to remember all the different ways in which personal judgment will necessarily *still* be exercised. First, Rome requires him to "come home." But suppose, as his minister, I have required that he *not* go there, that he remain a faithful Protestant. Now, who makes the decision between these two competing authoritative voices? Who decides which voice is not *genuinely* authoritative?

And incidentally, there are far more than just these two choices. Countless other groups beckon him as well. In all this, the ultimate decision will be made by the person making the decision. This means that this is a dilemma that cannot be escaped. If I were to be asked by a Roman Catholic how I know my private interpretation is correct (over against the hubbub of all other private interpretations out there), I can reply with the same question. "Assume for a moment that we agree that we sinners all have need of an infallible interpreter. How do *you* know that you have picked the right infallible interpreter?"

Second, if a man were to return to Rome, he would discover that he had not left the pandemonium of having to make choices in our Baskin-Robbins Protestant world for the plain vanilla solitary choice in the Roman fold. Multiple choices *still* confront him. These choices include what "denominational" faction within the Roman church he will align with. Will he be a Latin rite family, ultramontantists, middle of the road nearest Catholic church advocate, part of the "let's ordain women as priests" faction, cheerleaders for liberation theology, etc.? These are not hypothetical questions—there are choices to make, and the magisterium of the Church will not necessarily help make them. For example, the pope is unlikely to say, any time soon, that all nuns should leave the liberal Maryknoll order. And, if he *did*, the likely absence of subsequent discipline would lead many to believe that he didn't mean it. Authoritative teaching is impossible without authoritative action.

Third, let's assume that this convert does the normal thing and simply begins attending the local parish church. As he continues to read his Bible, he still has as many interpretive choices as he did when Protestant. The teaching office of the Church has not produced an authoritative set of commentaries on the Scriptures, verse-by-verse. A few key passages have been authoritatively interpreted, but that is all. When it comes to the vast majority of the Bible, he is still on his own.

Fourth, personal judgment has to engage in a strenuous effort to submit to the magisterium and "unanimous consent of the fathers" because the first thing it has to do is *find* it. In other words, there is a vast mountain of teaching and conflicting voices to sort through, and one thing the magisterium has not done is give us a table of contents to identify the precise boundaries of that magisterium. Where can I go and get a leather-bound set of all the infallible determinations of the Church?

For just one particular example, the *Catechism of the Catholic Church* says that Muslims as Muslims can be saved. "The plan of salvation also includes those who acknowledge the Creator, in the first place amongst whom are the Muslims; these profess to hold the faith of Abraham, and together with us they adore the one, merciful God, mankind's judge on the last day." (p. 223). So Muslims are said to worship the same God. Is this right? More importantly, is it part of the magisterium? If not, what is it doing there in the catechism? If so, then do you think it would be possible to find another authoritative statement from another era in Catholic history which contradicts this, *Unam Sanctam* for example? Is *Unam Sanctam* part of the magisterium? Who sorts these apparent conflicts out?

The Protestants have a defined rule of faith, the Scriptures. The Table of Contents is fixed; the Protestants are committed. But the faithful Roman Catholic is told that he cannot interpret the fixed Bible without the aid of non-stipulated, non-fixed magisterium. It is like being told that you cannot read the map rightly without being given the key—but then the key is hidden.

Fifth, assume that a Roman Catholic has a written document from the Church which is (beyond dispute) part of this magisterium. How does the individual interpret these words? If he cannot interpret the words of Scripture, then how can he hope to interpret the far more complicated words of, say, the *Catechism of the Catholic Church*? And if he can rightly interpret the words of the *Catechism*, then why can he not understand the book of Romans? The Catechism says "Christ's Resurrection is the fulfillment of the promises both of the Old Testament and of Jesus himself during his earthly life" (p. 170). Paul says that God declared Jesus to be the Son of God with power by His resurrection from the dead (Rom. 1:4). Why do I have the ability to understand (on my own) the first set of words from God, but I need help for the second set?

Sixth, personal judgment must be used in order to sort through disputes within the Roman Catholic church concerning the *meaning* of a particular place within the Church's teaching. For example, *Verbum Dei* says that since "therefore all that the inspired authors or sacred writers affirm should be regarded as affirmed by the Holy Spirit, we must acknowledge that the books of Scripture firmly, faithfully, and without error teach that truth which God, for the sake of our salvation, wished to see confined to the Sacred Scriptures" (Article 3, II). Conservative Roman Catholics point to this passage to defend their (correct) view of the infallibility of the Scriptures in their entirety. But liberals in Rome point to the same passage to show that the Scriptures are infallible on matters concerning our salvation. Who settles such disputes?

Seventh, personal judgment needs to frame the question before it rightly. The choice is not between the countless Protestant groups that hold to *sola Scriptura* on the one hand and then Rome on the other. The comparison must be made between equivalent formal principles. In other words, the first decision that necessary personal judgment must make is between groups that affirm *sola Scriptura* on the one hand and groups that affirm Scripture together with an infallible interpreter on the other. And if our concern is schism it should be noted that a far greater degree of unity exists between different groups that affirm the former than those groups which affirm the latter. Of course, once that choice is made, further downstream choices must then be made. Once Protestant, one must decide whether to be baptistic or paedobaptistic for example. But it is simply a category mistake to present the basic Roman approach as monolithic over against the fragmented Protestants.

With all this said, I would like to spend just a little time pointing to relevant Scriptures. We are told to emulate the Bereans. "These were more noble than those in Thessalonica, in that they received the word with all readiness of mind, and searched the scriptures daily, *whether those things were so*. Therefore many of them believed; also of honourable women which were Greeks, and of men, not a few" (Acts 17:11–12). Having heard the word preached from apostolic mouths directly, the Bereans turned to the law and the testimony.

Paul commands the Galatians to exercise personal judgment if apostles or angels show up teaching anything contrary to the true *depositum fidei* (Gal. 1:8–10). The Word they had already received was authoritative, and the Galatians were commanded to hold fast to the understanding they had once had, regardless of the rank held by one who contradicted it. Paul also tells the Thessalonians to "*prove* all things; *hold fast* that which is good (1 Thes. 5:21). This is not a scriptural anomaly. "I speak as to wise men; *judge ye* what I say" (1 Cor. 10:15). We find this kind of exhortation in many places. "Let *no man* beguile you of your reward in a voluntary humility and worshiping of angels, intruding into those things which he hath not seen, vainly puffed up by his fleshly mind" (Col. 2:18).

The apostle John also expects believers to have their wits about them, and to use them. "Beloved, believe not every spirit, but try the spirits whether they are of God: because *many false prophets* are gone out into the world" (1 Jn. 4:1). The same thing applies when dealing with itinerant missionaries with bad credentials. "If there come *any* unto you, and bring not this doctrine, receive him not into your house, neither bid him God speed" (2 Jn. 10)

Jesus speaks the same way: "Beware of false prophets, which come to you in sheep's clothing, but inwardly they are ravening wolves. *Ye shall know them* by their fruits. Do men gather grapes of thorns, or figs of thistles? Even so every good tree bringeth forth good fruit; but a corrupt tree bringeth forth evil fruit" (Mt. 7:15–17).

When dealing with Gnostics and JWs, it seems that our duties are clear. But do we have to be careful lest our use of personal judgment lead to schism? Obviously, Scripture warns us to avoid both the sin of schism *and* the sin of unity. It would be nice if everything were simple, but alas, it is not. We are told to maintain unity in the strongest possible terms, and we are also commanded to separate from error in terms equally strong. How can both these requirements be observed? How can we submit to the *ministerium* of the Church, and at the same time exercise personal judgment? The Bible gives us the parameters. "*Obey them* that have the rule over you, and *submit yourselves:* for they watch for your souls, as they that must give account, that they may do it with joy, and not with grief: for that is unprofitable for you" (Heb. 13:17). We are to obey them. Obey them as they do what? As they build on the essential foundation. "And are built upon the *foundation* of the apostles and prophets, Jesus Christ himself being the chief corner stone; In whom all the building fitly framed together *groweth unto* an holy temple in the Lord: In whom ye also are builded together for an habitation of God through the Spirit" (Eph. 2:20–22).

Every humble piece of wood in the building must reject false carpenters. Every living stone has the responsibility to reject spurious stone masons. "*Cease, my son, to hear* the instruction that causeth to err from the words of knowledge" (Prov. 19:27). This is true personal judgment. Such injunctions can be obeyed by us—it is not an impossibility. Humble personal judgment can be made to sound like arrogance, but only if we say that comparable passages in the Bible are also arrogant. "I have more understanding than all my teachers: for thy testimonies are my meditation. I understand more than the ancients, because I keep thy precepts" (Ps. 119:99–100).

Some last few objections, and then I'll be done with this point.

Personal judgment has been abused.

Granted. What glorious thing hasn't been? This would include marriage, alcohol, tradition, and more. We have to distinguish between righteous things which can always be abused in a fallen world (like wine), and those things which in themselves are an abuse (like drunkenness).

Personal judgment has led to the chaos of the modern divided Church.

Why do we say this? Why do we not go back a step further and say that Rome's refusal to acknowledge lawful personal judgment made it impossible to exercise godly personal judgment within the fold of the Church? This objection is a version of the *post hoc* fallacy, and says that since the modern fragmented world came after the Reformation therefore the Reformation caused the modern fragmented world. Why do we not say that the Renaissance popes were the culprit? The schismatic is the one who actually *caused* the schism. John the Baptist didn't have a cushy office set-up at the Temple. He preached in the wilderness, but this did not make *him* the schismatic separatist. *They* were all back in Jerusalem.

Personal judgment has done more divisive harm than good.

Here I simply issue a flat denial. No, it hasn't. While I agree that the divisions in Christendom are greatly to be lamented, I would also say that the situation is not as bad as it is frequently portrayed by Roman Catholic apologists (e.g., "25,000 Protestant denominations"). The actual figure is much lower—and most likely comes from David Barrett's *World Christian Encyclopedia*. As of 1982, he identified seven major ecclesiastical blocs, and some 22,190 denominations fall under these seven blocs. The first bloc is Roman Catholic, which contains 223 denominations. The Orthodox give us 580. Non-White Indigenous gives us 10,956. Anglicans account for 240. Marginal Protestants (Mormons, JWs, etc.) add up to 1,490 denominations. (Non-Roman) Catholics give us 504 denominations. Coming in at #2 would be the Protestants with 8,196.

But wait, we're not done. This Protestant figure counts (necessarily) independent Baptist jurisdictions, so that if a city has seven different independent Baptist churches, this counts as seven different denominations. The same skewed effect happens with the 194 Latin-rite denominations. Countering this optical illusion, Barrett goes on to break the seven major ecclesiastical blocs into what he calls "major ecclesiastical traditions," where I think we come up with an accurate number. So that I don't bore the patient reader, let me just focus on the division of three of the major blocs. The Orthodox are divided up into *nineteen* traditions, the Roman Catholics have *sixteen*, and the Protestants have *twenty-one*. If we throw the Anglicans in, they account for another six.

Far from Bedlam, this appears to be simply the cost of the gospel doing business in a fallen world. But whichever door you choose, you have lots of work for personal judgment to do in following up that choice.

Finally, at the final day of judgment, God does not count by twos or tens. Each individual will stand before Him to give an account, and if that individual sat under the ministry of lies, then that individual will be judged accordingly, and all in full accordance with the Scriptures.

CHAPTER VII

Becoming Hindu
in Beverly Hills

I recently heard a very nice gentleman give his testimony about his pilgrimage from various forms of evangelical Protestantism to Eastern Orthodoxy. He was obviously sincere, intelligent, well-read, and spiritually hungry for God, but I was really concerned about the central hinge in his argument.

Before getting to that, I am including this in a book on Roman Catholicism even though I know that Eastern Orthodoxy considers Rome and Geneva simply two sides of the same western coin. In many ways this is true, but in other ways (this one included) RC and EO are two sides of the same coin. The hinge I spoke of is the one created by varying interpretations from multitudes of people, and the apparent safe haven that EO presents for those who are tired of the storms caused by all these private interpretations.

After his talk, I presented my question to him in several different ways, and he did not seem to understand my question at first. But as we talked, he appeared to get what I was pursuing, but was still not able to answer the question. This was unfortunate because it is a question that everyone has to answer, and not just evangelical Protestants.

It goes like this: The problem he faced as an evangelical was caused by the various and contradictory doctrinal "grids" he had adopted over the course of his life, and at the end of the day he realized that all he had was a "just me and my Bible" approach. He didn't have "just the Bible" (what he thought was the doctrine of *sola Scriptura*), which sounded reliable, but rather he had the Bible and his own private understanding of it. So in his hunger for something outside himself, he began to read the early church fathers, and was bowled over by what he read. From this fascination with the church of the first millennium (which he did not think existed anymore), he finally came across Eastern Orthodoxy and identified it with what he had been reading.

But notice what happened. He moved from recognizing that private interpretation of the epistle of Romans was "inadequate," but then fully trusted himself to his private interpretation of Ignatius, Polycarp, Irenaeus, et al. He read these men and thought he had a reasonable idea of what the early church was like, and it was all done with "just me and Ignatius."

He had been in a world where all the evangelicals he knew read Romans differently, and this unsettled him. But how does this hermeneutical dilemma disappear just because we moved from interpretation of Scripture to interpretation of church history or the early fathers? Yes, there *are* many voices claiming to understand Scripture, and yes, they contradict. But to throw up my hands and step to the right three paces, take down another book, and undertake the interpretation of something else (far more inchoate and difficult) *does not solve the problem at all*. If I can't read and understand Romans, then I can't understand Irenaeus either. And if I can't understand Irenaeus, then I can't understand the ecumenical councils, which are ostensibly there to guide me through Irenaeus (and the other fathers, and Scripture). How can I read the councils? How can I tell if Eastern Orthodoxy has fallen away from the determinations laid down in the Definition of Chalcedon unless I can read and understand what Chalcedon says, and read and understand what Eastern Orthodoxy is saying? Suppose someone says that I just have to trust the Church, and I should listen to my priest, letting him handle it. Okay. How am I supposed to understand *him*?

Suppose I am standing here as a good Protestant with my Bible, having just read Romans, and someone approaches me and says that I can't trust what I come up with there because I was looking at it *with my own eyes*. He then hands me a book that contains what he would like me to believe. But instead of reading it, I should be a little more wary and rather ask, "Do I have to read this *without using my own eyes*?" If I get to use my eyes with *his* book, then could he please go over what the problem was supposed to be with my reading Romans? But if I don't get to use my eyes with his book, the objection is being consistently applied across the board, but now I have no way of knowing what he is trying to tell me. In other words, private interpretation is inescapable. And to point to its existence (and its problems) among evangelical Protestants is completely beside the point.

When this gentleman had read the early fathers, he had taken them in a particular way. But just about every church father he mentioned I had also read and had come away with a different interpretation that he had. And the Roman Catholics have scholars who are no slouches when it comes to patristics, but they have a different take, a third one. This can be multiplied many times over. During the Reformation, the most notable patristic scholars in Europe were the Reformers, not the Roman Catholics. That emphasis is part of what the Reformers meant by *ad fontes*, back to the sources.

Now if we are not to trust the Bible because of "all the interpretations," it seems that it would follow that we are not to trust the church fathers either—because there are so many interpretations. We are not to trust church history because there are so many interpretations. We have RC church historians, Mennonite church historians, Reformed church historians, and Baptist church historians. If the argument is sound, then we ought not to trust church history.

Okay, so we need an interpretive community. Fine. Which one? And who decides which one? At the end of the day, the searcher has to trust his own judgment when he is determining which interpretive community to trust. We have RCs, EOs, confessional Presbyterians, Copts, Armenian Orthodox, Byzantine

Rite, Lutherans, and on and on, over the horizon. In other words, despite the efforts to make it appear otherwise, no one of these communions is privileged when it comes to the basic hermeneutical issues. These communions are not outside the interpretive clamor. They are not "above the fray." And the individual, in the presence of the God who will judge the hearts of men, is the one who has to decide.

One last comment: For many evangelicals who are attracted to these communions, it is not so much a powerful attraction to an embodied culture as it is dissatisfaction with their own inadequate embodied culture. As evangelicals, they have been trained to (always) yearn for "something more." Something deeper, richer, more profound. And in our context, it is easy to be attracted to a particular form of worship that promises much. But we really should be more careful. To take a basic example, a preacher may be fluid, and eloquent, and persuasive, but those listening to him should really want to know how he lives at home with the wife and kids. In other words, is what he is saying persuasive to *him*? In the same way, as we are considering these issues, we should want to take note of how these ancient communions have embodied themselves incarnationally over time. What does this kind of faith do when it has had the run of a place for ten centuries? Those who are considering conversion should exercise due diligence and move to a small island off Greece (for Orthodoxy) or a mountain village in Mexico (for Roman Catholicism) and see what life is actually like there. What happens when there are no outside influences messing about with this form of worship, over the course of centuries? To do anything else is really too much like converting to Hinduism in Beverly Hills.

CHAPTER VIII

Authority and Clarity

Oftentimes, those considering conversion to Roman Catholicism tell me they want to emphasize a distinction between organic and incarnational Christianity on the one hand and propositional Christianity on the other. In those situations, I feel a little like Paul in Jerusalem when he was asked to continue to remember the poor, the very thing he had come there to do (Gal. 2:10). Obviously, I can't speak for every Protestant congregation, but I *can* say that we here in Moscow have been living and emphasizing an organic and incarnational approach to the Christian faith for many years.

Now the irony is that all faiths (provided they last more than one generation) are organic faiths *de facto*, despite what they may say in their creeds. The propositional assent is given at the required time because this is their organic tradition. This creates a problem for them because the propositional creed sometimes collides with the organic reality at periodic intervals. The only way to keep a faith propositionally pure is to adopt a hard-line sectarian mentality, which has been done for a short while. But if the sect lasts more than one generation, organic realities always take over. People in differing groups will say, "Hail, Mary!", "the five *solas*!", or "Great is Diana of the Ephesians!" for the same organic reason: it is part of their life.

The faithful and scriptural ideal is to have the organic life and the truth taught about that life from the Word line up. I agree with that completely: life first, then dogma. And let me note in passing, concerning the *life* of most of these wannabe Roman Catholics, that they and their family are *organically* Protestants. They are members of a Protestant church, their children attend a Protestant school, they have Protestant friends, they labor with Protestants in business, and so on, into countless other areas. The teaching of our church to such a person is that they should take all this organic life seriously and incarnationally—our dogma lines up with their life (and ours). Such men are currently entertaining propositions that would take them, if obeyed, to the organic setting of another communion. This is why we should agree here that propositions and organic life can be distinguished but never separated. Every organic action can be propositionally expressed. But it is important to emphasize that such a person would *not* be leaving a "propositional" church, and their departure *could* be explained as obedience to a mere proposition—"The church I was in was not the true Church."

And as I see it, the conversion such men are contemplating undermines the organic connection of the covenantal history of the Church prior to the coming of the Lord.

When I have brought up the Bereans, who turned to the law and the testimony to evaluate a direct apostolic word, I have been told by those intrigued by poping that the Bereans "were not evaluating 1500+ years of Church history, but examining the new teaching of the gospel in the light of the revelation of the Law and the Prophets." But "Church history" is *precisely* what they were examining. This new teaching of the gospel was being established over the stiff resistance of the rabbis. I've been told that the Bereans were examining the new, not the old, but it is more complete to say that they were examining the new over against those who wanted to maintain the venerable traditions of the fathers. With regard to what was *claimed* by their opponents, they were evaluating 1500 plus years, right back to Moses and before. Surely everyone would agree that church authority prior to the coming of Christ was organic, not propositional. The New Testament did not usher in an era of organic religion, supplanting the older propositions.

Related to this, I have also been told that John the Baptist did not start a rival Temple. But actually, in a sense, he did. He was the *forerunner* of the rival Temple. Jesus was the one who tore down the existing Temple and promised to replace it in three days. The old ways, the traditions of men, the ancient practices, the glorious Temple, all went up in smoke, and it was the pleasure of God. And what does Rome have in her claims that Jerusalem did not have, too?

But to return to the first example, how can the Bereans examine this way without placing themselves in the position of final authority? I've been told, "It seemed to us that, in the realm of Christianity, personal judgment inevitably requires an authoritative Church to avoid becoming individual judgment." This is correct in what it states, but wrong in what it assumes. We agree that an authoritative church is necessary—a church as such that outranks individuals as such. But an authoritative church is not the same thing as an infallible church. Of course, if *infallible* simply means nothing more than the right to put certain subjects off limits for debate, then the word *infallible* has collapsed to mean merely *authoritative*. But of course, this means that a non-Catholic church is "infallible" too—so long as infallibility is flexible enough to mean fallibility. I am not trying to abandon my irenic spirit here, but…I don't know how to deal with this kind of thing without calling it sophistry. Don't we have a scriptural infallible infallibility over against a magisterial fallible infallibility?

Allow me to highlight this with an illustration. Three neighborhood children live in three neighboring houses—the Smiths, Millers, and Johnsons.

The Johnson kid is out of control, and shows no respect for the requirements of his parents. We shall call him Individualist Johnson. He is out back in the garage, holding a revival meeting, and so we need not disturb him again.

The Smith kid wants to be obedient (desperately) but his parents are dysfunctional and have created for him a mass of practical (*organic*) contradictions. He is R.C. Smith.

The Miller kid wants to be obedient too, and his parents are comparatively average—right sometimes, wrong sometimes, and potentially wrong at any given time. His name is P. Miller.

Now, let's say that in a discussion with the Miller kid, R.C. Smith postulates that his parents are not only his authority, but that they are infallible. P. Miller concedes that parents are authoritative, but he says that at any given point they are capable of error. This does not diminish their authority, but rather it shows P. Miller's high view of it. For example, he is willing to submit to a decision that he believes is in error, but does so simply because his parents have required it. R.C. Smith thinks that this shows a low view of parenthood, and says that his parents are infallible—but only sometimes. This infallibility comes and goes. He says that he is required to submit to his parents' infallible decisions, but that he is free to question their fallible ones.

Now, the most reasonable question in the world for Miller to ask is how to tell the difference between the decisions. When are his parents being infallible? When not? This is not carping or criticizing—it is a practical organic question. If Miller wants Smith to go swimming with him, it matters whether or not Smith's parents have said that he could, or that he could not, or both in a contradictory way, or that he could not (but this decision could be questioned by the son), or that he could not (and it cannot be questioned by him), and so on. The boundaries of true authority matter to the submissive heart.

And this is where I believe those who are consider adopting Roman Catholicism back away from their "organic" commitment to authority significantly. It seems serious and high-minded to say "Obey your mother," but it is inconsistent with this injunction to then discourage any serious subsequent attempts to discover exactly what she has said to do. I've been told by such people that the "idea of the magisterium is that of a living body of authoritative interpreters of the deposit of revelation—the primary part of which is inscripturated in the Bible. It is quite misleading to consider it merely as the collection of writings left by the magisteria of the past, although these too are part of the magisterial gift to the Church at large," and so on. However, a commitment to "order, charity, and submission" remembers what it was told to do yesterday, and the day before that. If I am diligently laboring to obey my mother, and she told me last week that Muslims were all eternally lost and she tells me this week that they are worshipers of the true God,[9]

---
9 *Catechism of the Catholic Church*, The Holy See [http://www.vatican.va/archive/ENG0015/_INDExod.HTM, accessed July 2015], par. 841.

then what is my organic obedience supposed to look like? If I think she is fallible sometimes and infallible sometimes, this spares me from having to assert an ultimate logical contradiction, but it does not help me decide which is fallible and which is infallible *at all*.

I've been told, "Many of the problems [raised] deal with the propositional identification of the magisterium, rather than its organic reality. The primary relationship of the Catholic with the magisterium is through the living Bishops of his day. The historic magisterium is important, but the living magisterium is the working point of contact. If there is a problem, and you identified several areas worthy of discussion, the answer is to discuss it with the current members of the magisterium . . ." But there is not a "problem" requiring discussion here. The Catechism I quoted concerning the Muslims was intelligible enough, and I had no questions about what it meant. It was very clear. The imprimatur was by Joseph Ratzinger, former Pope Benedict, and the Holy See reserved all rights to itself. My only question is whether this Catechism is part of the magisterium. If so, then why not just submit to it? Why discuss it at all? But you say, rightly, that there *is* debate. This is because, apart from the assertion that it does speak with a single voice, this authority does *not* speak with a single voice. And if the Catechism is *not* part of the magisterium, then what would it take for something to become part of the magisterium? In short, there is debate on such things within the Roman Catholic church because the point I am making about the magisterium is clear, which is that the boundaries of said magisterium are unclear.

I am not writing these things because I need more precise propositions in order to make all my syllogisms happy. I am saying that submission to authority requires clarity. A geometrician in Euclidville wants clarity. Enlightenment philosophies pursue clarity, it's true. But despite propositional idolatries, obedient sons also desire clarity—but for a completely different reason.

SECTION THREE
THEOLOGY INCARNATED

CHAPTER IX

Four Kinds of Idolatry

Richard Baxter once said, "It is almost incredible how much ground the devil takes when he has once made sin a matter of controversy: some are of one mind, and some of another; you are of one opinion and I am of another." Nowhere is this more apparent than when we discuss the use of images in prayer. We are given straightforward commands regarding this, but the commands go contrary to something that runs deep in the human heart, and so it has become controversial.

The apostle John warns his children to stay away from idols, and he does this because (presumably) it was possible that true Christians might not want to do so (1 Jn. 5:21). This being the case, we should distinguish various kinds of idolatry. For my purposes here, I am understanding idolatry as placing a created thing where only the uncreated God should be. This clearly happens whenever images are used in prayer, but images need not be involved. Idolatry is more subtle than that.

1. Idolatry without images. The apostle Paul tells us in an aside that covetousness is idolatry (Col. 3:5). This means that the objects of a man's covetous desire have come to occupy the place of devotion in his heart that only God should occupy. We don't think this happens only if the covetous man starts burning votary candles in front of his bankbook. The fact that this idolatry is "low church" doesn't keep it from being idolatry. And given the nature of covetousness, we can see that idolatry can extend to anything—if your neighbor can have it instead of you, you can covet it (Exod. 20:17). And when you do, that's idolatry.

Idols of the heart are really hard to smash. The heart is deceitfully wicked, and is fully up to the challenge, for one example, of fashioning even iconoclasm into an idol. When that happens the idol leers from his intellectual shelf in the temple of reason, as much as if to say, "Get me *now*."

This kind of covetous idolatry doesn't need images, but it is not surprising that it still kind of likes them. Do covetous people pour over catalogs, full of *desiderata*? A godly woman looking at a catalog is shopping. A covetous woman pouring over a catalog is worshiping.

Incidentally, this is why the use of porn is clearly idolatry. The covetousness is right there, which is idolatry. And whatever icon you click on your desktop, it ought not to be an image of a man bowing down before a buxom Astarte.

2. Idolatry as traffic with false gods. The Scripture clearly teaches us that it is also idolatry to worship false gods (who are really there) with images. "Turn ye not unto idols, nor make to yourselves molten gods: I am the LORD your God" (Lev. 19:4). In this instance, the problem is not the images, the problem is what they represent. The gods themselves don't mind those images; they encourage them. The images truly represent the false.

In biblical vocabulary, false gods are not the same thing as non-existent gods. There were spiritual realities behind these images.

"As concerning therefore the eating of those things that are offered in sacrifice unto idols, we know that an idol is nothing in the world, and that there is none other God but one. For though there be that are called gods, whether in heaven or in earth, (as there be gods many, and lords many,) But to us there is but one God, the Father, of whom are all things, and we in him; and one Lord Jesus Christ, by whom are all things, and we by him" (1 Cor. 8:4–6).

Paul is saying that for believers there is only one God. He acknowledges that there are "gods many and lords many" out there, but in the biblical parlance, these are demons, not divine beings (1 Cor. 10:20). Demons are not non-existent. At the same time, they are not what they claim to be. The clearest instance of this is when Paul casts a spirit out of a girl at Philippi (Acts 16:16). The Greek says that she was possessed with the spirit of a python, making her a devotee of the god Apollo. Or, as a Christian would say, demon-possessed.

With such idolatry, the images are not rejected because they are inaccurate, but because they are accurate representations of terrible gods. For the idolater they are accurate because they open up the way to "spiritual realities," which they really do. For the faithful believer, they are accurate because they are impotent wood and stone (Is. 44:15), which accurately represent the ultimate impotence of the spiritual realities behind them (Ps. 115:5).

3. Idolatry as superstition. I don't want to spend a lot of time here, because this is not a significant biblical category. But suppose someone made up a little Mother's Day Goddess, or used a Hummel figurine to represent the "spirit of recycling" or something in their morning NPR meditations. These things would have no spiritual realities behind them and are just dumb. But they would still be idolatry—at a minimum they would be idolatry in my first sense.

4. Idolatry as the worship of the true God through images. Note what Aaron says when he convenes a festival around the golden calf.

"And he received them at their hand, and fashioned it with a graving tool, after he had made it a molten calf: and they said, These be thy gods, O Israel, which brought thee up out of the land of Egypt. And when Aaron saw it, he built an altar before it; and Aaron made proclamation, and said, *To morrow is a feast to the* LORD. And they rose up early on the morrow, and offered burnt offerings, and brought peace offerings; and the people sat down to eat and to drink, and rose up to play" (Exod. 32:4–6).

So we may distinguish the worship of false gods with true images (#2) and the true God with false images (#4). But this is not a distinction between idolatry and non-idolatry. The Bible condemns them both and in the same terms. When the people of Israel were prohibited from making images, they were prohibited from making images of the true God as much as anything else in the creation that they might bow down to in the name of a false god (Deut. 4:12).

We know this because when Paul discusses the golden calf incident, he calls this worship of YHWH *idolatry*. "*Neither be ye idolaters*, as were some of them; as it is written, The people sat down to eat and drink, and rose up to play. Neither let us commit fornication, as some of them committed, and fell in one day three and twenty thousand" (1 Cor. 10:7–8).

So the apostle Paul condemns a certain form of YHWH worship as idolatry. What? Because of the presence of the calf, not because of the absence an invocation of YHWH. This means that people who worship Jesus Christ, the true God, in the form of images, are still guilty of idolatry.

Having discussed four kinds of idolatry, let us proceed to ten theses on idolatry.

1. Those who object to portraits of Jesus should not have various Christological heresies assigned to them. It is as if a ham-fisted painter tried a portrait of my best friend, and I complained the painting had no soul. The painter could not reply that I was saying my friend had no soul. But we are talking about his painting, not my friend. We are talking about the

painter's artistic inadequacies, not my friend's soulless inadequacies, which is probably why the painter keeps trying to change the subject.

2. The historic doctrinal errors of the first wave of iconoclasts cannot be assigned to the Protestant objections to them, any more than the errors of iconoclastic Islam can be assigned to Protestants. At the same time, sin begets sin, and sin invites overreaction. The errors later ratified by Second Nicea were and are responsible for the judgments brought in by Islam. Christian idolaters lost what the gospel had gained. Protestants understand the overreaction, just as they understand the provocation of it. That does not make them participants.

3. The Incarnation was a momentous event, but provides no new argument for icons that didn't exist before. There were plenty of Old Testament theophanies concerning which the current arguments for icons would work equally well. But still the Jews did not use images of the Lord walking in the garden with Adam, or of Abraham serving dinner to the Lord and two angels, even though all such events were not visions, and were photographable. They were visitations, and to deny the lawfulness of portraying the visitation is not to deny the visitation. It is to *affirm* it. To pick up a brush with a claim

you can reproduce what happened is to deny what happened.

4. We don't know what Jesus looked like, thank God. There are no descriptions of Jesus in the course of His earthly ministry from which we may take any kind of direction. Had cameras been invented at that time, we would no doubt have some interesting discussions about *that*, but they would not be the discussions we are having now. Our discussions now concern the work of untethered and uninspired imaginations, and not a record of what actually happened.

5. Speaking of first century cameras, the Lord in His great mercy to us kept them from being around at the time of the Incarnation. But had they been invented, I am prepared to say that Mary could lawfully have taken her family album out from time to time to remind herself of the Lord's presence with them, just as we do with our photos. But if she had had one of the photos enlarged at Kinkos, and set up a shrine for it, then that would have been wicked.

6. The descriptions of the Lord in glory that we do have (hair white like wool, feet as burnished bronze, flaming eyes, and a sword coming from His mouth) are word paintings intended to serve the

only purpose we need to have, not to provide grist for another purpose.

7. There is a difference between a painting that attests to the *fact* of the Incarnation (e.g., Road to Emmaus) and an attempt at a portrait. To deny the former as lawful could lead some to draw false conclusions about the Incarnation (i.e., that Jesus never quite "touched down"—some form of docetism). But attempts to capture the reality of the *personality* of Jesus in a painting, or by an actor in a Jesus film, or by a novelist in attempted dialogue, reveal next to nothing about Jesus, and reveal a great deal of the manifest coxcombery of artists who are not nearly as good at their craft as they think they are. It makes me think less of Jesus in an edifying way, and more about how some artistic types could spend a couple days in the stocks in an edifying way. BBC producers notwithstanding, a vaudeville cloth lion is not Aslan.

8. God said not to do this in the Second Commandment (Exod. 20:4–5). Convoluted arguments that "we can too do it" need to spend at least some time showing what is being prohibited by this commandment, instead of constantly arguing what is still allowed by it. I understand that blue pomegranates in the Temple curtains are not prohibited by the Second Word. What is prohibited? What

tendency in the natural man is being affronted by this prohibition? Unconverted men want to lust, they want to steal, they want to hate, and so God speaks His holiness into a sinful world. So what is it that unconverted men want to do with images? What holy word does God speak into a sinful, *religious* world? He says not to bow down before an image in religious devotion.

9. The commandment to honor parents is the first one with a generational promise, and which the apostle Paul points to (Eph. 6:2–3). But it is not the first commandment with a generational rider. The Second Word says this—that those who bow down to images are guilty of "iniquity," and that their hatred of God will be visited to three and four generations (Exod. 20:5). In our worship of the Lord, we delight to include our children together with us in our worship, and this includes bringing them to the Table. But it is not enough to just include your children. *What* are you including them in? We do not bring them into a worship service with graven or painted images in it because we do not want a millstone tied around our stiff necks (Mt. 18:6). We do not want to be thrown into the depth of the sea. We want to present ourselves to the Lord at the last day, together with the children He has given us.

10. Idolatry is a grievous and soul-threatening sin, and not a denominational distinctive. An ability to follow and understand these arguments is spiritually given, and cannot be apprehended by those who are still natural men. This is why the new birth is absolutely necessary.

CHAPTER X

Take the Blue Pomegranates, for Example

It is perilously easy to read your own practices and assumptions back into the history of the Church. This anachronistic impulse is universal, and much of the time it is merely funny and endearing, but when it is elevated to the point of dogma and insisted upon as a religious duty, the problems that result can be serious.

As an example of mild anachronism, consider the portrayal (in countless Sunday School curricula) of Adam and Eve as a suburban, white American couple sans clothing. This, in spite of the fact that everyone knows that Adam and Eve were Chinese, and that all the other races developed from this primal race . . . or maybe not. But the likelihood of Adam and Eve looking just like your neighbors next door in Cleveland is remote.

But the more serious examples of anachronistic reading are found when one branch of Christendom claims that what they are currently doing is what has been consistently done from the time of the apostle Paul on down. There are certainly Protestants who do this; there are even some who claim that Paul, in an amazing miracle, used the King James Version of the Bible. "*We* do this, *we* are the apostolic band, and therefore it follows that the apostles used to do whatever it is we are currently doing."

Having said this, there are two central arguments against the use of images in the worship. The first is that the Bible plainly says not to worship in this way. The second is that the early Church did not worship in this way. Claims that they did worship this way are simply anachronisms, comparable to the claim that the first Christians used to give an invitation to come forward at the end of the service to receive Christ. No, that particular technique was invented by Finney in the 19th century and to project it backwards in time cannot be sustained by the evidence.

In the same way, to take the action of the Second Council of Nicea, which settled the use of images in worship, as normative for the whole church is to project onto the early Church practices which would have appalled them all. Differences between Christians who claim the early Church used icons and Christians who claim the apostles used the King James Version are differences of degree, not of kind.

The Protestant claim here is that Scripture flatly prohibits the worship of images in the Second Commandment. And, as I have said earlier, the Second Commandment trumps Second Nicea. The Second Commandment reads this way: "Thou shalt not make thee any graven image, or any likeness of any thing that is in heaven above, or that is in the earth beneath, or that is in the waters beneath the earth: Thou shalt not bow down thyself unto them, nor serve them: for I the Lord thy God am a jealous God, visiting the iniquity of the fathers upon the children unto the third and fourth generation of them that hate me, and shewing mercy unto thousands of them that love me and keep my commandments" (Deut. 5:8–10).

As we can readily see by comparing Scripture with Scripture, this is not a prohibition of the making of images, but rather a prohibition of images that you then bow down to or worship. Images generally are fine, even images for decoration in a religious context—blue pomegranates, say. Cherubim on the ark of the covenant are just great also, because the whole point was to studiously avoid bowing down to them, and rather (like them) to bow before the mercy seat where there was no image at all. So the issue is not images. The issue (the *only* issue) is images as an aid to religious devotion. Don't. Nyet. Nein. *No*.

The reason given for avoiding this practice is God's jealousy. Now what is jealousy like, especially divine jealousy? Is a jealous husband likely to be mollified if his wife admits that she was *physically* batting her eyes at another guy, but nowhere does the Bible explicitly say that eye-batting constitutes unfaithfulness or adultery? No, jealousy is generally operative *at the perimeter*. Jealousy is activated by how it looks, and not just by what it may become later on.

The response is that all this was altered at the Incarnation. Jesus was a particular person, with particular features. Those who knew Him during His sojourn here on earth could recall what He looked like. The Incarnation (if it means anything) means that if cameras had been invented in that day, it would *not* have been unlawful to take a picture of Christ. He was really there. John emphasizes this in the opening words of his epistle. "That which was from the beginning, which we have heard, which we have *seen with our eyes*, which we have *looked upon*, and our hands have handled, of the Word of life" (1 Jn. 1:1). What they were seeing, and looking upon, was the icon of God, the Lord Jesus. Having said this, given the idolatrous nature of the heart of man and all its devious little twistings, we may thank our God above that cameras had not been invented then. If they had, we would be dealing with every manner of cargo cult now.

The fact that God took on human flesh in the Incarnation (a miracle He was competent to perform) does not mean that we have the ability to recapture that miracle in any paltry representation of ours—whether done by shutter, brush, hammer and chisel, or an interpretative dance junior high troop performing *Godspell*. The fact of the Incarnate One two thousand years ago does not automatically protect any and all aspiring actors and artists from aesthetic impudence.

> Only take heed to thyself, and keep thy soul diligently, lest thou forget the things which thine eyes have seen, and lest they depart from thy heart all the days of thy life: but teach them thy sons, and thy sons' sons; Specially the day that

> thou stoodest before the Lord thy God in Horeb, when the Lord said unto me, Gather me the people together, and I will make them hear my words, that they may learn to fear me all the days that they shall live upon the earth, and that they may teach their children. And ye came near and stood under the mountain; and the mountain burned with fire unto the midst of heaven, with darkness, clouds, and thick darkness. And the Lord spake unto you out of the midst of the fire: *ye heard the voice of the words, but saw no similitude; only ye heard a voice.* (Deut. 4:9–12)

So in the older covenant, God revealed no form to the Jews, and made a special point of reminding them of it. There were other instances in the Old Testament where there were forms revealed (the angel of the Lord, Ezekiel's wheels, the Ancient of Days, and so on) but when it came to the question of worship, God went out of His way to reiterate with them that there was no form shown to them on the mountain. In another instance, when the people had been told to "look to" the bronze serpent, over time this looking became devotional looking, and Hezekiah had Nehushtan destroyed. To which we should respond, good for old St. Hezekiah, patron saint of the righteous iconoclasts.

So what about my earlier claim that the use of images is anachronistic? This is all related. Consider again the history of God's people. God gave them the prohibition of images at the time of Moses. This was obeyed throughout the days of Joshua, but Israel's relationship with this commandment was pretty rocky thereafter. They struggled with this, their besetting sin of idolatry, for centuries. Finally, because of their idolatries, they were taken into Exile. Now, after the Exile, they finally had the prohibition of images in worship *down*. Other problems developed (of course) because not all idols are made out of wood, stone, or paint, and Jesus certainly rebuked the ideological idols of the scribes and Pharisees. But at least they were fierce about keeping material icons and idols away. And this they should have done without neglecting the weightier matters of the law.

Now after our Lord has risen from the dead, and the gospel began to be preached among the nations, the first nation to receive the word was the Jewish nation. And while the nation as a whole rejected Christ, many thousands of Jews believed in Him. St. James says that many thousands had believed, and they were all zealous for the law (Acts 21:20). They kept "the customs" (v. 21), and needed to be reassured that Paul did also. What do you think? Does anybody here think that these customs included candles and prayers in front of pictures?

It is granted that their zeal was focused at that moment on the question of circumcision, but here is a little thought experiment. Do you think that these Jewish Christians, zealous for the law, used icons in their worship services? If you do, your powers of imagination are far greater than mine. The epistle of James identifies the believing synagogue of James 2:2 with the church of 5:14. I have used this argument before when talking about the inclusion of infants in our churches. The idea of excluding them would have been *absolutely alien* to the believing synagogues in Judea.

In the same way, the veneration of icons in a Christian synagogue in A.D. 57 would have gone over like a big pile of greasy bacon at their men's prayer breakfast. And this example provides us with an *a fortiori* argument because the bacon was even explicitly declared okay at the first great church council. That was one of the changes made between the covenants, and it took the decision of a church council to make it even halfway palatable.

My argument here is that the veneration of images was not one of the changes between the old covenant and the new, and if it *had* been one of the *intended* changes, it would have taken seventeen church councils to bring it about, with fifteen of those councils occurring while all the apostles were still alive and able to attend. And the New Testament would have been a lot thicker. The reason that the use of images in worship was not controversial in the first generations of the Church was because nobody was doing it. Centuries later, when they began to do it, the controversy came.

Not bowing down to an image was not just a matter of "oh, okay" obedience for the first Jewish Christians. Because of the history of the previous centuries, it had gotten to the level of a deep and godly prejudice, down in the bones. It was taboo, like kissing your sister. You just don't do that.

This prejudice was picked up by the Gentile Christians. The believing Jews did not abandon their suspicion of images; rather, the Gentiles coming to faith embraced the Jewish loathing of them. This is the more remarkable because most of these Gentiles had grown up with the use of images in worship. The God-fearers among the Gentiles had been attracted to the worship of the synagogue precisely on these grounds.

The gospel was preached to the Gentiles, with this feature of the Christian faith as one of the great selling points. "Forasmuch then as we are the offspring of God, we ought not to think that the Godhead is like unto gold, or silver, or stone, graven by art and man's device. And the times of this ignorance God winked at; but now commandeth all men every where to repent . . ." (Acts 17:29–30). And they did repent, and the Gentile world streamed to Christ as presented in the preached gospel and enacted Eucharistic meal. No images. It was some centuries before the innate human desire for a god who won't talk back was able to mount a comeback.

For those who want to worship as the ancient Church did, I would urge them to do better than the eighth century A.D. Go much further back, go back to a believing synagogue in Judea, a synagogue that worshiped Jesus as the Messiah, in 57 A.D. If you can find a painting there that was used as an object of religious veneration, I would be happy to eat it. But I still would not bow down to it—because whether or not this particular argument is any good, my God is still a jealous God.

Citing the Second Commandment (Exod. 20:4–6), Dr. Paul Owen (on the podcast Communio Sanctorum) asks, "Does this commandment forbid physical demonstrations of veneration before images, and the adoration of the Eucharistic host in the worship services of the Church? I do not believe it does." Since I *do* believe that it does, let me mention just a few brief responses to some of Dr. Owen's reasons.

First, he argues that the context of this commandment is "plainly dealing with the temptation to worship false gods." He goes on to note a number of things about the commandment that are quite obviously true. "They are to give their allegiance to YHWH alone. They are to demonstrate that allegiance by refraining from making images of foreign deities."

Now it is quite true that the Second Commandment prohibits graven images of false gods. But it is equally true that it prohibits graven images of the true God. Not only does God warn the Israelites in Deuteronomy 4 to remember that they saw no form on the mountain (which would prevent them from trying to make an image of the true God), we also see in Aaron's brief excursion into idolatry in the golden calf incident. Aaron made the prohibited image, but he did not do it in order to worship pagan deities.

When he saw that the people were worshiping the calf as another god, he built an altar in front of it and declared a festival to the *Lord* (Exod. 32:5). But he was tumbling down a mountainside in an avalanche, and was trying (futilely) to steer the three ton boulder bouncing in front of him. And when he came down off the mountain (in a very different way) Moses was not prepared to try to understand any nuances. He called the Levites to his side (v. 26), and in a display of remarkable divisiveness, not to mention hurtfulness to the work of global ecumenicity, he sent them out into the camp to take out about three thousand of their fellow Israelites. And they were blessed that day for doing so. Their targets would include revelers who were worshiping the calf, those who were not worshiping the calf but who just like to dance, those who were not worshiping the calf but saw a real opportunity to get laid, and the delegates from the National Council of Churches who were busy ministering at the altar Aaron made in the shadow of the golden calf. At moments like this, nothing is lamer than Aaron's excuse—"out came this calf." And I don't want to be caught with a lame excuse like that when the Lord comes back. I don't want Him to appear when I am in the middle of kissing an icon. Of course, Dr. Owen is right that we may not worship false gods in this way. But neither may we worship the true God in this way.

Dr. Owen points out what he believes to be a key distinction between pagan idolatry and the use of images "in some expressions of modern Christianity." He says that "images of deities were viewed by the ancients as actual, sentient, bodies of the gods." He goes on to say that this "is not the way those who venerate images in the Church are supposed to think of them." But there is a confusion here, and it is found in that word "supposed." In all idolatrous cultures, a distinction can always be found between those philosophical minds who have a sophisticated understanding of it, and the guy in the street who does not. Where can we find more gods than in street-level Hinduism, but in philosophical Hinduism all is one. Sure, there is a difference between a rank superstitious approach and a sophisticated approach. Part of our discussion of this issue earlier addressed the superstitions that crowd in on the people generally on the basis of rationalizations that intellectuals can follow, but which no one else can. More than one person in the world thinks they have a real spiritual presence with them, and they "don't care if it rains or freezes, long as they have their plastic Jesus, riding on the dashboard of their car." It is not sufficient to simply wave our hands over it and say that they are not "supposed" to do that. What happens to them if they do? Why does the bishop encourage it? Why are the *crude* mailings that I have seen (wear this medal with true devotion and you will be ten feet tall and bulletproof!) sent out with the approval of the Church? Why aren't the Levites strapping on their swords? Um . . . just to be perfectly clear, the previous sentence was a metaphor.

Two more points. Dr. Owen says, "Images of Christ are images of the seen God (Jn. 1:18). They are images of God's own image of himself (Col. 1:15). They are not attempts to image the ineffable divine nature." This is quite true. But they are attempts to make an image of something that God has already made an image of. Christ is already the icon of God. Why should we make icons of *the* icon? When the disciples were talking about the life of Christ ten years after the ascension, can you imagine one of them saying, "No, no. That was in Galilee. Don't you remember? Jesus was by the lake and He pointed to Andrew, and . . ." In this, when one witness was recalling an event to other witnesses of it, there was absolutely no need for them to all deliberately shut out of their minds any remembrance of what Jesus had looked like on that day. "Second Commandment, you know!" John deliberately recalls what he had seen and touched (1 Jn. 1:1–3). But for anyone who had encountered God's icon in the flesh to try to sub in their own attempts at it would be more than a little weird. I believe Paul refers to this when he says, "Wherefore henceforth know we no man after the flesh; yea though we have known Christ after the flesh, yet now henceforth know we him no more" (2 Cor. 5:16). Because of the Incarnation, we affirm that Christ came *in* the flesh, and that He remains a true man forever at the right hand of God. But there is a way of knowing Christ *after* the flesh that St. Paul walks away from. And I would submit that devotion in front of inanimate objects is an example of that kind of thing. So, I affirm that first century cameras were in principle lawful and that a snapshot of Christ would have been lawful also, and yet I would also say that if I were in possession of such a snapshot, with its own certificate of authenticity, the Second Commandment would still prohibit me from bowing down to that picture. Why? We do not know the enfleshed Christ after the flesh.

Dr. Owen concludes by saying that he believes that the equivalent offense would be when the gods themselves are conflated. "The equivalent sin of our day would be to conform the identity of the one true God to the teachings of other religions—whether it be the God of Judaism, of Mormonism, of Islam, or of Protestant liberalism." I happen to agree that to conflate the gods in this way is also a violation of the first two commandments. But of course, the problem is that while this is also occurring, the spirit of syncretism that drives it is also at work in much of the ecumenical movement, and pushing in the same direction, for the same reasons. The Spirit of the Age has gotten into the ecclesiastical kitchen and is trying to cook up a vat of indiscriminate goo.

CHAPTER XI

Let's Go Kiss Us Some Icons

I recall one time, back in the day, when I was having a discussion with my dear wife about what I was going to wear for preaching attire. This was back in the Jesus people period. At issue was whether or not I was going to wear jeans with or without the patches. Not surprisingly, Nancy was urging the latter and I was inclined to the former. One of the reasons I advanced for my choice was that I did not want to get "on the road to Rome."

Seems ludicrous now, but this is how arguments from "trajectory" work. Given the penchant for organization displayed by the human mind, which is in its turn a reflection of how God made the world, it is impossible to leave one error without heading toward another one. It is not possible to leave an error forcefully without creating a situation in which you are forcefully headed toward another error. This situation arises *whenever there is any motion at all.*

If we are called to walk on the old paths, and we are, then this scriptural illustration makes it clear that there are two ways to disobey. We can veer off to the right or to the left, and we are commanded to do neither. "Ye shall observe to do therefore as the Lord your God hath commanded you: ye shall not turn aside to the right hand or to the left" (Deut. 5:32).

So if you grew up in the left ditch, there is no way to urge repentance, asking your companions to come with you back to the road, without looking to *them* as though you are arguing for life in the right ditch. To further complicate matters, and because the devil is a clever fellow, some of those that you *do* persuade to come with you back to the road will take the first opportunity that presents itself to tumble into the right ditch, all while giving you a bunch of the credit. Then you have deal with them, and their arguments, along with taunts from the left ditch behind you. "See? *See?*"

There is no road to Rome. Rome is across the road, in the other ditch. But we should worry less about the ditch they are in and more about the ditch *we* are in, and our responsibility to stay on the road once we have regained it. Our basic responsibility to the right ditch is to stay out of it—and not to taunt those in it. I'm still covered with mud from the left ditch and to accuse others of right-ditch-muddery doesn't seem fitting somehow. At the same time, it is crucial to recognize what is going on with the right ditch and to recognize the temptations presented to us by any movement away from the left ditch.

At the time of the Reformation, the encrustations of medievalism were the left ditch, and the anabaptists were the right ditch. Anabaptism and other forms of radicalism are where you went when you overshot. This is why the Reformers had to fight the anabaptists as they did, and this is why Rome blamed the Reformers for the anabaptists. But today, after centuries of individualism and enculturated anabaptism here in the left ditch, Rome (and EO) have now become the right ditch. This means the work of *true* Reformation will deal with left-ditch conservatives and right-ditch this-is-*so*-much-better-than-where-we-were-ism.

One of the things the Reformers did, and did very well, is that they "assumed the center." But there is no way to do this without incurring the dual charges that you are facilitating the way to right ditchism, and also that you are still, at the end of the day, tragically attached to the left ditch. But enough of the history lesson.

One of the ways we can tell a real work of reformation is occurring today is by the reactions to it. Sound doesn't travel in a vacuum, and reformation does not occur without immediate noise and clamor from *both* ditches. When you talk about the Spirit's work today, in your home Bible study group there in the left ditch, be prepared for someone to say, "Beware, beware . . . the Spirit, as you call it, could land us all in the right ditch. We are quite comfortable here. *Sola fide*."

"But," you say, "I am not urging us to go there at all. Scripture forbids . . ."

Just then another member of your group pipes up to say, "Yay! Let's go kiss us some *icons*!"

Lest all this seem a little oblique, let me spell it out. When men slander us as being on the road to Rome, that is what it is—slander. When others praise us for being on that same road, and thank us for having pointed out the road signs to them, the disapproval is gone but the *slander* remains. If one man falsely accuses me of being a thief, and I deny it, should I take comfort from someone else who praises me for having the quickest fingers he ever saw? When a hidebound TR hears Tridentine echos when I am quoting the Westminster Confession, and a budding young papist hears the same thing, then they are both exhibiting the same degree of theological sharpness, which is to say, the sharpness of a pound and a half of wet liver. The sharpness of a bowling ball. The sharpness of a small pile of our living room couch cushions. You get the drift.

So the Lord has shown us the way, and we should walk in it. Distractions will make their appeals from both right and left. That's what distractions do. Let us ignore them, shall we? The work of reformation lies before us.

CHAPTER XII

As the Ankle Bracelet Gets Itchy

Discussions of the doctrine of imputed righteousness often act as though the whole momentous subject swirls around a mere handful of texts, and as though the doctrine is not assumed in virtually everything Scripture says about the relationship of a holy God with sinful man. It reminds me of how geologists can find evidence of local floods all over the world but the idea of a global flood is an alien concept to them.

For those who accept the basic doctrine of the sinfulness of man (establishing the need for justification) and the existence of a holy God (establishing one who justifies), there are only two basic directions you can go. You can either assume that justification occurs as God infuses righteousness into us, or you can believe that it occurs as the result of righteousness being imputed, credited, or reckoned to us as a forensic act.

The doctrine of the Roman Catholic Church takes the former position.

> The first work of the grace of the Holy Spirit is conversion, effecting justification in accordance with Jesus' proclamation at the beginning of the Gospel: "Repent, for the kingdom of heaven is at hand." Moved by grace, man turns toward God and away from sin, thus accepting forgiveness and righteousness from on high. "Justification is not only the remission of sins, but also the sanctification and renewal of the interior man."[10]

The quotation at the end of this citation is from the Council of Trent. Justification is understood to be the remission of sins (which the *Westminster Confession* also affirms), but is also described as the renovation of the inner man. When a man "accepts" righteousness from on high, he is accepting it into himself. Westminster agrees with the part about forgiveness, but everything else is radically different.

---

10 *Catechism of the Catholic Church*, Part 3, Section 1, Chapter. 3, Article 2, I.

> Those whom God effectually calls, He also freely justifies; not by infusing righteousness into them, but by pardoning their sins, and by accounting and accepting their persons as righteous; not for any thing wrought in them, or done by them, but for Christ's sake alone; nor by imputing faith itself, the act of believing, or any other evangelical obedience to them, as their righteousness; but by imputing the obedience and satisfaction of Christ unto them, they receiving and resting on Him and His righteousness by faith; which faith they have not of themselves, it is the gift of God.[11]

Note that the issue is not whether there is a renovation of the inner man, which all serious Christians believe, but whether that renovation is to be understood as our justification. And of course, it cannot be.

For the Protestant, justification is a declaration in a courtroom, and it is the just declaration of "not guilty," pronounced over a very guilty sinner. Now how this is possible—how God can be both just and the one who justifies—is vindicated by the high wisdom of God, and it is vindicated by means of imputation. If we succeed in dismantling the concept of imputation, we find at the end of the day that we have dismantled our only possible hope of salvation.

---

11 *Westminster Confession of Faith* 11.1.

If the "not guilty" pronounced over me consists of my state of sanctification in "the interior man" (which is very imperfect indeed), then this means that my justification is at best a work in progress. But I don't need a work in progress—I need a definitive declaration, and to be told by the bailiff that I am free to go. Anything less and I am not actually justified. I am just on probation, walking around town being followed by a censorious parole officer, and the ankle bracelet is starting to itch.

The prisoner in the dock who hears the words of the gospel is a man who hears a glorious "no condemnation" in the first words of Romans 8. Later on in that chapter, he is the same vindicated defendant who is now able to throw taunts at all the lawyers in the prosecutor's office who are trying to dig up additional dirt on him. "Who shall lay any thing to the charge of God's elect? It is God that justifieth" (Rom. 8:33).

The reason I can be declared not guilty without God Himself ceasing to be just is because God reckons me to be represented fully and completely by my Head, the Lord Jesus. Not only so, but He represented me in the condemnation that I suffered in Him, and He represents me currently at the right hand of God the Father. "For he hath made him to be sin for us, who knew no sin; that we might be made the righteousness of God in him" (2 Cor. 5:21). This kind of thing can only happen by infusion or by imputation, and it can't really be done by infusion. That narrows things down a bit, and we discover that the Holy Spirit has backed us into a good news corner.

There are three imputations that are an essential part of all this. The first is the imputation of Adam's transgression to all of us. Then there is the imputation of all our transgressions to Christ. And last there is the imputation of Christ's righteousness to those who have faith in Him. Now the reason imputation works—in all three cases—is that the human race is not made up of solitary and disconnected individuals.

If we were entirely distinct individuals, then it would make no moral sense at all for God to let me go free because there was an entirely innocent guy over there, and all that was necessary was for God to kill somebody, preferably somebody innocent. This is another case of great Sunday School illustrations actually being instances of high moral monstrosities. An evil twin is hauled before the court, and his good brother volunteers to take his place on the scaffold. What kind of judge would say, "Hey, *that* sounds like a plan to me"?

The human race is constituted as a race. Individual persons are not like individual rocks in the driveway, but rather like individual leaves on a tree. Each leaf can be made out distinctly, but anybody who seeks to understand leaves without reference to the tree is not following the path of wisdom. So when Adam and Eve were in the Garden, the whole human race was there, and in Adam the whole human race threw itself over the precipice of sin. When Christ died on the cross, the entire new human race was represented there in Him, and when Christ obeyed God throughout the course of His life, the new human race was there, in Him, represented (justly) by His obedience. Imputation works with us because human beings are defined by imputation. Imputation is a forensic, legal and covenantal action.

God has created us as a covenantally integrated unity. This is why imputation is not an outrage—if the imputation is between a covenantal, federal head and those represented in and through him. If we tried an imputation of righteousness (or unrighteousness) between Smith there and Murphy here, everyone would be rightly appalled. You don't impute the characteristics of one leaf to another one. Everybody knows that.

I said earlier that the textual issue is like a vast series of local floods that somehow are not seen to add up to a global flood. Here is a passage that struck me on this subject recently:

"And be found in him, not having mine own righteousness, which is of the law, but that which is through the faith of Christ, the righteousness which is of God by faith" (Phil. 3:9).

There are many things that could be said about this, here and elsewhere (there are many local floods), but I am interested in one phrase only—Paul says he wants to be found "not having his own righteousness." Let us get one thing clear at the outset—if Paul is to be justified by righteousness, whose will it be? For starters, Paul says *not mine*.

Whatever else we say about justification, we need to fix it in our minds that we are put right on the basis of the righteousness of somebody else. There is absolute no other way to get to the liberation of no condemnation. And once we have been declared legally, forensically, covenantally not guilty, the Holy Spirit can infuse as much sanctifying righteousness as He wants, which is a great deal.

This is moral liberty—the opposite of antinomian licentiousness and the opposite of legalistic wowserism. It is a blast of mountain air after two hours in the sauna.

If you want a description of what the fruit of imputed righteousness tastes like, there is no better description than what C.S. Lewis provided:

We want, above all, to know what it felt like to be an early Protestant. One thing is certain. It felt very unlike being a 'puritan' such as we meet in nineteenth-century fiction. . . In the mind of a Tyndale or Luther, as in the mind of St. Paul himself, this theology was by no means an intellectual construction made in the interests of speculative thought. It springs directly out of a highly specialized religious experience; and all its affirmations, when separated from that context, become meaningless or else mean the opposite of what was intended . . . All the initiative has been on God's side; all has been free, unbounded grace. And all will continue to be free, unbounded grace. His own puny and ridiculous efforts would be as helpless to retain the joy as they would have been to achieve it in the first place . . . He is not saved because he does works of love: he does works of love because he is saved. It is faith alone that has saved him: faith bestowed by sheer gift. From this buoyant humility, this farewell to the self with all its good resolutions, anxiety, scruples, and motive-scratchings, all the Protestant doctrines originally sprang.[12]

---

12 C.S. Lewis, *English Literature in the Sixteenth Century* (Oxford: Oxford, 1973), 32–33.

CHAPTER XIII

Theology With the Chambermaid

The distinction between the magisterial doctrine of *sola Scriptura* and the modern, individualistic *solo Scriptura* is, in my thinking, straightforward. *Solo Scriptura* maintains that the Bible is the only authority over "me," and, fortunate for "me," I am the only interpreter of the Bible who has any credibility and weight with "me." In other words, *solo Scriptura* is "just me and my Bible." And, human nature being what it is, it is not long before we wind up with "just me."

By contrast, *sola Scriptura* does not claim that the Bible is the only religious authority in the lives of believers. Rather, the claim is that the Bible is the only religious authority in the lives of believers that has the two particular characteristics of infallibility and ultimacy. Infallibility means that Scripture, as the very word of God, does not make mistakes, does not err. It is *the* ultimate standard of what is right, and so I must always conform myself to it and not go the other way around. I must not bend the Scriptures to fit what I (or others that I know) think might be more accurate, that accuracy determined elsewhere.

As an aside, one of the reasons why conservatives retreated to the word inerrancy was because liberals, bless their hearts, had begun nuancing the word "infallibility" to mean something more akin to "fallibility." They would also do such things in the name of "honesty." I am using the word infallibility in its older sense.

Ultimacy means that there is no court of appeals past the Bible. This is how I am using the word *absolute*. Biblical absolutism means biblical ultimacy. I do not bring other standards to evaluate Scripture; I am not to weigh the Bible in the balances of biology, astronomy, clinical psychology, oral legends, the book of Mormon, lexicography, or philosophical and rudderless Frenchmen.

I can (and must) bring other standards and authorities to bear to help me understand what the Scriptures are actually saying. The Bible teaches that I am as a Christian to submit myself to spiritual authorities other than the Bible. These authorities would include my parents (who taught me to love God before I could read), my church (which taught me, for example, to memorize Scripture), and Bauer's Lexicon (which teaches me that *eulogeo* means to bless). But none of these genuine authorities in my life are ultimate or infallible, which is fine, because authority is not an all or nothing proposition. However, without the touchstone of an ultimate and infallible authority located at the top of the hierarchy, all lesser authorities will wither and die.

With regard to the communion of the saints, this is something that we confess every Sunday as we say the Creed. So what are we talking about? First, the *context* of what we are talking about. The context is a universe teeming with intelligent life, celebrating the goodness of God and riches of His grace. Contrary to the notions of Enlightenment materialism, we do *not* live in a universe that is mostly empty space, punctuated here and there with dead rock or flaming gas. Many educated Christians have mostly gone along with this materialism, and are now trying to defend the last ditch, which would be the reality of the soul within man. I do not think they will fare well because they long ago took spiritual man out of the only habitat where he can flourish, which is a spiritual world.

But the problem is not Protestantism vs. Catholicism here—the culprit is education in Enlightenment terms. And you will find as much accommodation on such points among educated (indoctrinated) Roman Catholics as you will among educated (domesticated and tenured) Protestants. Perhaps even more accommodation. Take the theory of evolution for example. Who has kept opposition to *that* particular Enlightenment folly alive? Conservative Protestants. The holy father in Rome sees no tension between evolution and the creation account in Genesis.

Now this believing view of the universe can be simplistic and superstitious (as it has been in backwater parts of Spain and backwater parts of Tennessee), but it also has educated and erudite exponents (C.S. Lewis, for example). But it has to be insisted that the tendency to desacralize the world has nothing inherently Protestant about it. It *is* an inherent tendency of Enlightenment indoctrination centers, and yet when the problems start to appear, I see a lot of people suddenly becoming chary of their

Protestantism—but never of their graduate degrees, which is where the problem actually arose.

Now in a world that has *not* been desacralized, what does this do to our devotional life, both personal and corporate? When the psalmist exhorts everything that has breath to praise the Lord, this presupposes (given the boundaries and nature of poetry) that all these things have the capacity to praise the Lord (which I believe) and not that they have the capacity to read and sing that particular psalm (which I do not believe). As a minister, if I cry out in a call to worship that the galaxies should bow down, (as a good Protestant) I am not presupposing *anything* about my relationship to those galaxies, and (as a pre-modernist) I *am* presupposing everything about those galaxies and their relationship to their Creator.

The twenty four elders in Revelation represent the Christian Church, and the Christian Church presents her requests to God. We should assume that every servant of God is directed *by Him* to serve and worship Him in a coherent manner. Individual saints in glory (individually and corporately) may or may not know anything about us. We are not given any information on that score. But we know that they are praying for and longing for the day of redemption just as we are, and that their prayers line up with ours. This is God's department.

But if *I* single one of them out to submit my prayer requests to, then given the nature of the case, I must be doing two things. The first is what I discussed before—I must assume that he hears me. It is not enough to assume that it is *possible* that he hears me. If I have a choice (in a moment of danger) between praying to God in the name of Jesus, knowing that I will be heard, and praying to St. Thomas, not having any assurance that he will hear me at all, then I will pray to God every time. The only way I would ever pray to a saint is with the bedrock assumption that my chances of getting through are just as good as if I pray to God in the name of Jesus. And this leads to the second point that I did not touch on before. I also have to assume that the one to whom I am praying has a better "in" than I do. I have to assume a distance between God and me that the Bible does not encourage me to assume at all. Quite the reverse. If I pray the way the Bible instructs me to pray, then it makes no sense to afterwards turn to a lesser prayer, with a lesser mediator.

One other thing. We are taught in many places that God is a *jealous* God. His *name* is Jealousy. We should be exceedingly wary of any refined arguments (and any learned distinctions sliced lengthwise) that would bring us to the point where we could provoke that jealousy. God is jealous, and He is jealous with regard to this question of worship (of which prayer is an important part). The fact that humans can have it all worked out in their abstract theology (latria, hyperdulia, and dulia) such that they can admit to being an icono*dule*, but not an ido*late*r, makes me hop in place in my impatient Protestant way.

Imagine a wife catching her husband kissing the chambermaid. "Ah, my dear," he says. "I was meaning to talk to you about this. This is not what it appears. This is a species of what I have learned to call lesser-kissing. It doesn't *mean* the same thing to me as when I am kissing you—kissing you, my love, my dear, my only sweet, is what I call special-kissing."

"It may not mean the same thing to you," she says, jealous and angry as she should be. "But it means the same thing to *me*." And so she throws an expensive vase at his head, demonstrating an unwillingness to master some of the finer points of his theology.

CHAPTER XIV

Heavenly Prayer Requests

The question really is not whether the Roman church has a nuanced position on Mary that acknowledges that Christ is a "unique" mediator. I have no doubt that in the schematic catechism it would all be worked out carefully. They have done the same thing with the word *worship*—latria, hyperdulia, and dulia. This goes here, and cannot go there, and so forth. The whole thing is covered on paper. My problem is that when we bring it down from the realm of abstractions, what actually happens in the world where regular people pray? What actually happens is that people render "worship" to creatures that is *on a practical level*

indistinguishable from the worship they render to God, and this is the definition of idolatry.

Which brings us to the question of the communion of the saints and of Mary's mediatorial role. A standard question that is asked of Protestants is, "don't you all pray for each other?" What is the difference between saint A praying for you and saint B? Why do we privilege saint A in this matter just because he is alive and made it to your Wednesday night prayer meeting? Why cannot deceased saints join in with the prayers?

The answer has to do with the assumption that is being made when a prayer request is offered to a deceased saint, or to Mary (also a deceased saint). When I ask my friend Bob to pray for me because I have an appointment with the surgeon tomorrow, I do not have to assume any superhuman powers on the part of Bob in order to make the request of him. I know he heard me, because he was right *there*, and he heard the prayer request on exactly the same principles in play when he heard me ask him to pass the mashed potatoes. But when one person is caught in a storm at sea and cries out to Mary, and another at the same moment is struggling with his personal finances in Australia, and asks Mary to pray for him, this cannot be done *without assuming that Mary has all the functional attributes of Deity*.

Now it would not rock my Protestant world at all if I died and went to heaven, only to discover that at some point in my worldly sojourn, Mary had stumbled across some aspect of my story and prayed for me. "Oh my. Look at that poor sap *there*." But for me to *ask* her to do this assumes that she has a relationship to the world, and to everyone in it, including me, that Scripture does not give me any basis for believing. Of course I do not believe that departed saints cease to love their friends and brothers back here on earth. So the issue is not whether the saints in heaven can pray for Christians on earth. Why would they not be able to? This is part of the communion of saints.

The issue *is* what we have to assume about them in order to ask them to do so. And what we have to assume is that they can hear us. We do not have any encouragement from the Bible for believing this, and if we just go ahead and do it anyway, we are failing to make an important *practical* distinction between God who hears my every thought, and my Uncle Leonard, now with God, who does not.

The communion of saints means that the body of Christ is a glorious and unified mystery. It means I am one with all the saints in heaven, just as I am one with all the saints alive today in China. But if I were crossing a street, saw a truck with no brakes hurtling toward me, and cried out, "Wang Tu, pray for me!" my problem is simple to identify. I am assuming that the doctrine of the communion of saints gives Wang Tu greater hearing abilities than in fact he actually has. So the problem is not heavenly saints praying. The problem lies, not in the praying there, but in the prayer requests here.

If I assume that the saints in heaven can hear my thoughts, my murmured prayers, my unspoken requests, and what I write down, then I am necessarily assuming that from *my* perspective, I cannot distinguish their abilities from God's, at least as far as those abilities touch me. Since I have no encouragement from the Bible to make such assumptions, and since such assumptions have done much superstitious damage in the church, it is my view that it is the responsibility of faithful Christians to stay far away from them.

One concluding note: Lurking in the background of all this is the assumption that God somehow isn't able or willing to readily hear and quick to respond when His children cry out to Him.

CHAPTER XV

Corporate Testimony

Protestant apologists should be very careful in representing the Catholic faith to others. In short, we ought never to maintain that official Roman Catholic teaching affirms what it plainly denies, or vice versa. In other words, apologetics ought never do battle with a straw man. The warning is a good one, and there are many who are involved in Protestant/Catholic polemics who should take it to heart, and this would include Catholic apologists who misrepresent the official Protestant position.

With all this granted, and in the spirit of this admonition, I think we need to take this to the next level. We have to take even greater care to compare like to like. In order to do this, we have to ask where the misrepresentations actually come from and, having answered the question, we have to ask if it really is a misrepresentation at every level. And this takes us into the matter of corporate testimony.

Take the standard evangelical chestnut that Roman Catholics believe they are saved by works and not by grace. Where does this come from? There is no disputing that this is a standard assumption among evangelical Protestants, but where does it arise? What is the source of it? I do not believe that this is widely believed because some cult-buster Protestant apologist was reading through the catechism of the Catholic church, found that they attribute our salvation to the grace of God, and then said to himself, "*That* won't sell to my radio audience! I'll have to change it!"

No, I believe the real source of this widespread "distortion" of the official position of the RCC is from Catholics themselves, and they come to us in two kinds. First, the evangelical Protestant world has a multitude of ex-Catholics in our midst. I am a pastor of a conservative Reformed church, and we have *numerous* former Catholics in our congregation—a lot of them. When you talk to these people about their background and upbringing, certain features jump out. One positive thing would be gratitude for the teaching that caused them to fear God and to respect holy things. But on the down side, there is a very common response of having felt distant from God, of having to earn approval from Him, and of having had no practical understanding of grace. I have one of the best church secretaries in the Western hemisphere, and when some of us have commented on how efficient she is, one of her joking responses has been to attribute it to "that Catholic guilt." Now there are a lot of these people in our midst, and it does not take much to figure out what makes the rest of us conclude that the RCC is a place where "works righteousness" is taught. This is a constant refrain we hear from the steady stream of ecclesiastical refugees. This is not an incidental point.

Second, evangelicals are all about sharing their faith, and this has resulted, over the years, in numerous conversations with rank and file Catholics. These were not debates with the monsignor over what the official position was, but rather with pew Catholics over what made *them* tick. And many of us have heard the same kind of thing in those settings.

Now I know that the official Catholic position does not deny the possibility of a "personal relationship with God through Christ." Nor do I deny that there are practicing Catholics who have such a relationship. But I *am* affirming that there is something about how the RCC is set up that has caused a major disconnect between these elements of their official position and what the rank and file believe. And as a confessional Protestant, I believe that what that "something" is would be other elements of the official RCC position. If we take incarnational theology seriously, the official position is what the people are actually doing.

Allow me to assert something else important here. I write this as an evangelical, and as someone who is confessionally Reformed. But this is not written in a partisan spirit, because I am fully aware of how these same dynamics of "disconnect" are at play in the Protestant world. I don't believe they are at the same levels (yet), but they are certainly there in disconcerting ways. And when we see examples of such a disconnect in our own ranks, the response should be to assume responsibility ourselves, renew our commitment to police our own ranks and not to blame outsiders who draw the wrong conclusions. This is what it means to have a good testimony.

For example, our church was in a very public battle a number of years ago with the intoleristas in our community, and this battle has been conducted on many fronts. In this controversy, different kinds of outsiders are looking at us, and drawing conclusions about what we are all about, what we are teaching and doing and saying. Now this is what I mean by corporate testimony. We are in a small town, and there are hundreds of us. These hundreds of people have an identity that is associated with us, and (in my view) the vast majority of them have a good testimony with those who are outside. But it also has to be confessed that a handful of our kirkers (as we call them) have gone out there and (I say this with deep affection for every bone in their heads) and done some idiotic things. When this happens, it happens in front of two kinds of outsider: our enemies who are eager for any new material, and then the people who don't really have a dog in the fight, but who are curious. Their only contact with us is through the individual from our ranks who, for some reason, has decided to step out, high, wide and handsome. "Huh," they think. "What *is* Wilson preaching on over there?"

It does no good to complain about this because *this is how God made the world*. Never argue with gravity. This is precisely why the apostle Paul was so eager to urge Christians to walk in a manner that was worthy of the calling they had received.

Outsiders will look at us, and render general by induction. If a sufficient number of outsiders have the same experience, the induction will become proverbial. When that happens, it does no good at all to point to a piece of paper.

Put another way, our respective confessions of faith are worth something only when they are lived out in practical ways, and result in a lived out commitment to holiness, kindness, love, and justice. In the realm of abstractions, in a classroom, sketched out on the blackboard, I would be happy to pit the Westminster Confession of Faith against the Catechism of the Catholic Church. But that, by itself, is an academic exercise, and if it happens in the classroom only, it does not matter who wins the debate. The task of all ministry is to get the truth of the grace of God into the lives of the people of God.

In the discussion of what it means to be a genuine Christian, and what it means to be a member of the holy, catholic, and apostolic church, neither side should be allowed to "retreat to the catechism." We as Protestants embrace our catechisms, but this embrace is only legitimately seen and evaluated in our lives, incarnationally. In other words, do our people *glorify* God and are they *enjoying* Him on the threshold of forever?

This principle relates to a common critique of Protestants, which is that we don't have a real sense of respect for hierarchy and authority. But as we examine all this, we have to remember we are not dealing with a paper battle between what the Westminster Standards say about ministerial authority and what the Catholic magisterium says about it. In both cases there, we have high views of ecclesiastical authority. They differ, but they do not differ on the reality of that authority.

But if we have learned this lesson of the absolute need for application, the need to deny any distance between orthodoxy and orthopraxy, we will view this question differently. We will not ask, "Where is obedience taught?" We will ask, "Where is obedience practiced?" Now where it is practiced, it will no doubt be taught, but where it is taught, it is not necessarily practiced. So we are talking about how ecclesiastical authority is played out in real life. What is the incarnational manifestation of it?

Another aside: I have been (and will continue to be) a rather severe critic of numerous winds of doctrine in the contemporary evangelical church. I believe many of these contemporary movements represent one bad disaster after another, and are simply our Protestant form of going to semi-Pelagian seed.

When Protestants drifted away from their original high Augustinianism, it was only a matter of time before the folly of man-centered religion began manifesting itself in bizarre ways. This has happened before, when the medieval church drifted away from *its* high Augustinianism. I believe this drifting is the ultimate source of the disconnect between lip service to grace in the documents and practical sense that "it's all up to me" in the day to day business of living our lives. Some efforts at self-salvation will be examples of a dignified "high piety" (going to mass every day) while others will be openly narcissistic (soaking up the therapy speak of the contemporary evangelical church). But all of it represents neglect of the overflowing *grace* of God.

So back to views of hierarchy. As a minister in a confessional Reformed church, I have a congregation that insists on substantive sermons from the Scriptures, and the congregation is devoted in its attempts to live out what is taught. There is a high level of commitment to the Scriptures, and as we teach certain things as biblically necessary, I do not see a vast disconnect. And when there is a disconnect, we seek to provide pastoral counsel and help. For example, we teach that parents are responsible for the godly education of their children, and we have near universal application of this through homeschooling and Christian schools. There are other examples, but we believe that there must be a high correlation between what we say we believe and what we actually do. But with all this, we do not have certain formal marks of church authority. I don't wear a collar, don't go by *the Rev.*, and so on.

Compare this to what must be described as the adamant teaching of the RCC, and what is actually lived out. Remember the issue is incarnation here, not paper. To take one striking example, I really don't really think that a discussion of commitment to ecclesiastical authority is complete unless we include in that discussion the question of how many American Catholics practice birth control. This is like the two boys in the parable; one says he will go and doesn't, and the other says he won't and goes. In the world of incarnational living, nothing is more apparent than the fact that what the RCC says is necessary is disregarded by rank and file Catholics as unnecessary.

What does all this mean for the task of apologetics across the Roman Catholic/confessional Protestant divide? I believe that simplistic Protestant apologists ought not to be grandstanding for the audience in the cheap seats. "Did you know that Catholics believe that the *sacraments* are *necessary* for *salvation*?" "What! No! Booo!" The problem here is that the Westminster Catechism asks how the sacraments are made effectual means of salvation. Now what? To play to the nickel seats this way simply reinforces some of our problems with baptistic individualism, which are not insignificant. At the same time, there *is* a nuanced understanding of incarnational theology that makes this a legitimate point. But I do not make the point as one who taunts. This is a problem created by the sinful human heart, not by the pope in Rome, and it is evident in our circles as well. But when it is evident in our circles we confessional Protestants need to be resolved to deal with it in an incarnational way. This means dealing with it much better than Rome has.

SECTION FOUR

CATHOLIC FUNDAMENTALISM

CHAPTER XVI

Calvin's Fundamentalism

American fundamentalism made a series of strategic mistakes in its battles with liberalism in the early twentieth century. In the first rank of these mistakes was the retreat from a full-orbed world and life view, where everything is understood to be under the authority of Jesus Christ. They held to the fundamentals of the faith, true enough, but retreated with them into a truncated personal space.

Because of this mistake, there has been a tendency among some Reformed thinkers to disparage the whole idea of "lowest common denominator" fundamentals. But that idea is actually inescapable, and we can find a clear expression of it in Calvin.

In his discussion of church unity, Calvin argues for the two marks of the Church being a preaching of the pure Word and a faithful administration of the sacraments. This, obviously, leads straight to a question of how "pure" the preaching has to be, and how "faithful" the administration of the sacraments has to be. Calvin answers with an appeal to the fundamentals. He says this:

> For not all articles of true doctrine are of the same sort. Some are so necessary to know that they should be certain and unquestioned by all men as the proper principles of religion. Such are: God is one; Christ is God and the Son of God; our salvation rests in God's mercy; and the like. [13]

Unless distinctions are made between greater and lesser matters of the law, or doctrines which are of first importance and others which or not, it follows that schism is either impossible or permissible at any time. If everything is of equal importance, then schism can occur over every little thing, because there is actually no such thing as a "little thing." Many ministers have received single-spaced

---

13 John Calvin, *Institutes of the Christian Religion* (Peabody, MA: Hendrickson, 2008), 4.1.12.

typewritten letters, with typing up the side margins, from the peculiar kind of individual who thinks this way. He has the spiritual gift of Rebuking, and if you have deviated from his interpretation of anything whatever, out comes the typewriter. In this view, nothing is tolerated.

But the flattening of scriptural teaching can have another effect also—where anything and everything is tolerated. Departure from a church is never permissible, because the only hierarchy of values is that of the church in question over any particular thing in Scripture, no matter how "important." We need to have high views of church unity as Calvin did, but with a view of Scripture which would applaud the Reformation. This cannot work unless we rank the teachings and commands of Scripture appropriately.

And we need to have a high view of that which of first importance without elevating everything to that honor, thus resulting in church splits over anything. ("Dear Pastor Smith, it is with grief in my heart that I tender my resignation from our church family. When my wife saw the poster with a blasphemous and pathetic attempt at humor in the church nursery, she was appalled, as was I when I went down to look at it. I wept in my heart. Is it really appropriate to put a sign over the cribs that says "We shall not all sleep, but we shall all be changed" (1 Cor. 15:51)? Surely you would agree that this is not what the apostle had in mind at all, and I am afraid . . .")

Calvin was a true fundamentalist, and he was the kind that I would like to be. He used the doctrine of the fundamentals as the basis for his argument in favor of genuine church unity. And that is just what we need in this hour—catholic fundamentalism.

CHAPTER XVII

The Real Action Is Elsewhere

Jesus told the parable of two sons who were told to go work in the vineyard. One said he would go and did not. The other said he would not go, and then went. "Which one was obedient?" Jesus asked.

Whenever I have written on Roman Catholicism and Eastern Orthodoxy it has certainly generated a lot of comments, and I cannot say it was what I was expecting. But if the subject is addressed with the foundational issues in view, it touches on far more than denominational questions, and perhaps that accounts for the interest. I am not trying to whack a hornet nest, but I am living, writing, and teaching as a Reformed minister. I believe what I do, and here is some of it, written down for your amusement and edification.

I am a classical Protestant, a high church Puritan, a sacramental Calvinist, and a soteriological Augustinian. This complex of views did not appear in the world in the last few years, but has been confessionally intact for centuries, and has had notable representatives and advocates in the long history of the church before that. And in living within this noble tradition, I want to believe what I affirm, and affirm what I believe.

So which way does it go? Does the gold sanctify the altar, or the altar the gold?

I am told that my Protestantism is "modern," but classical Protestants deny the theory of evolution root and branch, and John Paul II had no trouble with evolution. Who has accommodated with one of the central claims of modernity?

I am told that my Protestantism is inherently sectarian and schismatic, and yet the bishops of Eastern Orthodoxy have a labyrinth of intersecting jurisdictions and competing interests that are, well, frankly, Byzantine. We are told that the multitude of Protestant denominations cannot be what the Lord had in mind when He prayed for unity in John 17. All right, let us look at the disharmony and disfellowshipping that is pervasive across the Eastern Orthodox world. Is *that* what He had in mind?

I am told that my Protestantism has no cultural soul, but then I have to return to my work in establishing a classical Christian college in which we have the students studying numerous talented pagans, Catholics, Orthodox, and Protestants. And I have to say, glancing over the curriculum, when it comes to cultural contributions, Protestants have certainly managed to carry our end of the log. Shoot, I think we would have carried our end of the log if J.S. Bach had been our only representative.

I am told that my Protestantism is disconnected from the ancient church, but I belong to a confederation of churches, every member of which is required to have the Apostles' Creed, the Nicean Creed, and the Definition of Chalcedon in their confessional statements. Not only that, but all the elders and pastors in our churches are required to *believe* them. We are a tiny splinter presbytery, you say, and I admit it. There are not many of us. In fact, there are more Roman Catholic priests in some states of our fair Republic who don't believe *any* item in the Apostles Creed than we have ministers who believe them *all*. Those who are sons of Abraham do the works of Abraham, and those who are sons of the apostles should have the decency to exhibit some kind of family resemblance. I say councils err and have erred, but actually believe every word of Chalcedon, including *theotokos*. Another man says that they cannot err, being the authoritative decisions of the holy Church, but always finds a way to reinterpret his way into some kind of comfort zone.

I am told that my Protestantism is disconnected from the apostolic church, but since my youth I have been steeped in the words and instructions of the apostles. And I have had acquaintances in the so-called apostolic communions who had no idea what the apostles taught, never having read them.

My favorite papist, G.K. Chesterton, once said that a courageous man would be willing to attack any error, no matter how old it was. But he went on to add that there are some errors that are too ancient to patronize. If I might adopt his observation, and adapt it to make a similar point, I would like to do so. I admit that there is something ludicrous about a hardshell Baptist church with fifteen members in rural Arkansas holding to the view that the Roman Catholic Church is "a cult." But let us as Protestants deal with that sort of thing—let us police ourselves.

In the meantime, let me urge my friends in the communions of Rome or the East not to patronize in reverse. Not all Protestants are snake-handlers or telehucksters. Let us acknowledge what the magisterial Reformation actually contributed. Get a map of the world, and look at it from halfway across the room. Grant that I am about to make a *generalization*, and that I cheerfully grant a host of variables that I am not mentioning here. That said, look at every nation that came into the Reformed faith at the Reformation, or was planted by heirs of the Reformed faith. You are looking at the First World. Look at those nations that remained pagan, at least up to the last generation. You are looking at the Third World. Ask yourself, when we have taken account of all the other contributing factors like language, climate, natural resources and so on, should the religious faith of the populace be considered a significant contributing factor as well? Of course, which is part of the reason Adam Smith predicted that North America was going to be wealthy and that South America, rich in resources, was not going to be.

I am not advocating simple causation or simple-minded causation for that matter, as though I was trying to put the eight ball in the corner pocket. But cultural influences include the general faith of the people, and the fact remains that during their centuries Protestants built a world-class civilization, too significant to be patronized. I also acknowledge that apostasy is a very real danger for God's covenant people and that those who used to be deuteronomic head can and will become the deuteronomic tail—unless they return to the faith of their fathers. And *that* goal is one of the central objects of our church's ministry here in Moscow, Idaho. I am not interested in a spitting contest with Roman Catholics and Orthodox, but rather in calling Protestants back to their magisterial, historical, confessional heritage. But in the course of doing this, many (influenced by contemporary individualism and low ecclesiology) have misunderstood the nature of the task and think wrongly that we are headed to Rome. As I have said elsewhere, I went to Geneva and people thought I went to Rome, simply because both are significantly east of Atlanta. Because of this misunderstanding and distortion, I am unfortunately in the position of having to spend time distinguishing what we are doing from Rome and Orthodoxy. But this is really a sideshow. The real action is really elsewhere.

CHAPTER XVIII

All Over the Map

One of the problems that Protestants, Catholics, and Orthodox *share* is the problem of ignorance of patristic literature. Because of this ignorance, the subject (which is theologically and theoretically important to RCs and EOs) can be used to cudgel (of course in a friendly way) those Protestants for whom the subject does not rise to the same theological importance. That does not mean that such things are unimportant to Protestants, but they are certainly not important in the same way. But frequently, the cudgeler and cudgelee share one thing—they have not actually read the fathers in question.

But when you actually start reading in the early church fathers, one of the first things you discover is that they are *all over the map*, just like us. While some modern debates are unheard of back then, many of the basic issues (like the use of images in worship) *were* debated, then as now, with fathers on both sides of the debate.

So suppose that I, a sturdy Protestant who likes the Second Commandment, want to appeal to something beyond my own opinions when it comes to the use of images in worship. Of course, I could always appeal to Moses and the still hot tablets he brought off the mountain. But that is insufficient for some. The words of Deut. 5:8–10 are apparently nebulous, and require an interpretative authority smarter than me.

I could, if I wanted, appeal to Irenaeus of Lyons, talking about one of the more suspect elements of Gnostic worship. "They style themselves Gnostics. They also possess images, some of them painted, and others formed from different kinds of material; while they maintain that a likeness of Christ was made by Pilate at that time when Jesus lived among them. They crown these images, and set them up along with the images of the philosophers of the world that is to say, with the images of Pythagoras, and Plato, and Aristotle, and the rest. They have also other modes of honoring these images, after the same manner of the Gentiles." Apparently, Irenaeus took a low view of "the manner of the Gentiles," as did Moses before him.

Now the use of images in orthodox worship came from somewhere, and there were orthodox fathers who did not get the same kind of fantods that I get when thinking about images in worship. That is not my point here. My point is that this debate and these concerns did not arise for the first time in the aftermath of Reformation. Nor was it the case that all the iconoclasts of the early church could be lumped in with the doctrinal enemies of the Incarnation. For another example, here is Epiphanius, bishop of Salamis, who once said, "It is a horrid abomination to see in Christian temples a painted image either of Christ or of any saint." And whatever else Epiphanius was, he was not a fundamentalist hedge preacher from Arkansas.

CHAPTER XIX

Christ in the Participles

One of the standard ways to talk about the difference between a Roman Catholic approach to the Lord's Supper is to refer to altar versus table. This is helpful, but it can still be misleading. When this happens, the debate reduces to a contest between the Roman Catholic "real presence" and the Zwinglian "real absence." And this is because we have fallen for the assumption that the sacrament is either on the altar, or not. If it is, then it is an altar. If it is not, then what we see is a table.

But we have to distinguish between real presence and local presence. Christ is certainly present in the administration of the Lord's Supper (it is the

Lord's Supper), but we limit things drastically by asking whether He is locally present in the bread and wine, as they sit there on the altar (or table). And, having limited things in this way, if we answer a certain way, additional questions about the veneration of the elements naturally arise. If Christ is present *there*, then should we not do what we would all do if Christ were there? Wherever Christ is, Christ should be adored.

But Jesus did not tell us to watch and adore. He told us to take and eat, take and drink. And in our obedience, Christ is with us. Christ inhabits the obedience, and the bread and wine are not obedient. *Christ is in the participles*, in the eating, and in the drinking. Christ is present in His body, and we are that body. As we take the elements and do what we were told to do (which did not include bowing down to them, adoring them, etc.) we are taken by the Holy Spirit and are knit together with Christ and the rest of His body. The elements sitting on an altar by themselves are nothing, and do nothing. But the elements are the instrument that God uses to accomplish His purposes. In order for an instrument to do what it is intended to do, it is necessary to do with it what we were told to do with it, which is eat, drink, and believe.

To take the elements of bread and wine, and separate them from the sacramental action, the sacramental participles, is a mistake of the first order. It is to remove an animated thing from the animating principle, thereby killing it, and then worshiping it as though it were alive by itself.

Lest there be any confusion here, I would identify my position as a close variant of sacramental Calvinism.[14] This means that when the people of God assemble in the name of Jesus Christ, and one of their number says the words of institution, and they together offer the memorial of Christ's body and blood by eating and drinking, Christ is really present among them. He is present with them in the person of the Holy Spirit, and they are present with Christ in heaven by the power of the Holy Spirit. Christ is present in this series of events in a covenantal way that He is not present at other times. (I am not talking about omniscience; of course in that sense Christ is present everywhere and always). For those who approach this with evangelical faith, His covenantal presence is presence for blessing. For those who approach it with idolatrous unbelief, His

---

14 For those who want to pursue the subject further, I would recommend Keith Mathison's fine book on the subject, *Given for You* (Phillipsburg, NJ: P&R Publishing, 2002).

covenantal presence is presence for chastisement. Many at Corinth had even died.

Too often a Zwinglian critique of the Roman Catholic understanding says that we should not adore or venerate the elements because Christ is absent. "He is not here; why are you venerating?" I would say that we must not adore the elements because Christ is *present*.

CHAPTER XX

The Smell of Boiling Water

Unity is always unity in the truth, and there are two ways to screw this up. One is to ramp up your particular articulation of the truth to such a high pitch that the only ones joining your new denomination are the neighborhood dogs. This is the abuse of using the truth in such a way as to fight against the foundational purpose of the truth, which is to see us all grown up into the perfect man (Eph. 4:13–15).

The other error regarding truth is to see the folly of this first sectarian error, glibly announce that doctrine divides and that Christ unites. Right. Cool. Christ who?

This is the lowest common denominator approach to truth, one that has been very common in evangelical circles for the last half century, and which certain fuzzy thinkers within the ranks of Protestantism are now suggesting as a way forward in the next wave of ecumenism. Let's see if we can dilute the soup a little further, shall we? If we do that enough, then we are sure to attract non-believers with the smell of our boiling water.

There is another way. If I believe, as I do, that the Jews are going to be grafted back into the olive tree, I certainly am not going to stumble at the idea of Roman Catholics, Eastern Orthodox, and Protestants coming back together. It is a glorious hope, one which I look forward to. But this is a hope based on the promises of God, and it therefore involves much more than a group hug approach to doctrinal issues.

In the meantime, we are all still part of the early church, and here I am in the tribe of Benjamin. Some of my fellow Benjamites are my adversaries, some are allies, and some are co-belligerents. Up north, some of the tribe of Ephraim . . . well, some are my adversaries, some are allies, and some are co-belligerents.

I know how to work together with Roman Catholics and with Eastern Orthodox, and I also know how to draw a hard line against various idolatries over there and against evangelical mush-mongers over here. But how can you do that, someone is going to ask. How can you make distinctions like that? "They are *all* in the tribe of Ephraim . . . good men? evil men? These nuances are killing me."

It is pretty simple, really, so this will be a short chapter. The only RCs and EOs worth teaming up with in any venture are the ones who don't mind a Protestant being one.

CONCLUSION

Loyalty As Grace

In a recent debate with an atheist, I was asked why I was a Christian. I replied that it was because my mother had spanked me. But I admit that this needs to be filled out a bit, and when we do, we will discover that the explanation is relevant to our discussions earlier in the book regarding personal judgment.

I have asserted that to bring in an authoritative interpreter solves no problems at all. It fails to do so on two levels. The first is that we still have the problem of how to read and interpret the interpretations. The Scriptures are given to us in words, and interpretations of those words arrive packaged in words. If God can't make Himself clear to me in the book that He wrote, how can I expect that fallible (or purportedly infallible) humans can do so? At this point, we might learn from the words of the old country preacher—"this here Bible sheds a lot of light on them there commentaries." But I am not arguing here for solitary individualism in interpretation; we live in interpretive communities and in interpretive traditions. More about this anon, as I would have said if I lived when *anon* was in more common use.

The second problem is that there are a large number of authoritative interpretations, just as there are "it seems to me" opinions at evangelical Bible studies. To react away from the latter because *you* have to decide which one is right, and to go to a place where you have to decide which pope, patriarch, or bishop is right, is to change nothing whatever. This is the basic point I have made in this book and on my blog, and it attracted quite a bit of attention in the comments section.

Now, to push this into new territory. To insist, as I have, that private interpretation is inescapable is *not* to fill up that word interpretation with philosophical rigor. I was made to trust in the Lord from the womb, and from my mother's breast. As I was being brought up this way, an interpretive grid was being established in my heart and soul, and this was not because my mother was telling me about hermeneutical spirals when I was eating mashed peas in the high chair. So when I was growing up in an evangelical Christian home, with parents who loved me, disciplined me, taught me, and who lived consistent Christian lives in front of me, I learned one of the first lessons of epistemology, which is personal *loyalty*. Loyalty to my parents, loyalty to their God, who is my God also, loyalty to the church in which I was nurtured, and loyalty to the gospel which contains the words of my salvation. That is why I said I was a Christian because my mother had spanked. Now I acknowledge that later, when I grew to maturity and joined the Navy (which is not a bastion of righteousness) certain challenges were presented to me, both intellectual and moral, and I had to learn how to answer the questions and challenges. But I did so . . . why? Because God had poured His grace out upon me in the family I had grown up in.

This was brought home to me a number of years later when our youngest daughter was sitting on my lap (she was about two), and she was busily telling me all about Jesus, and the cross, and salvation. She was authoritatively telling me all about it, and it struck me with great force that on this subject there was not a thought in her head that we had not put there. She was simply "parroting," a critic might say. But a second thing struck me, with equal force. And that was that *this was a design feature*. God did not create us to grow up religiously neutral until we are twenty-one, and then stick us in a divine library so that we could make up our own minds "objectively." God intends for us to learn our religious convictions on parental authority, long before we have any way to defend ourselves against parental heretics.

Now we have rebelled against this because it doesn't seem fair to us and because we want to trust in our own native abilities. And it must be admitted that God requires us to walk away from the faith of our fathers when our fathers have bowed down to a false god. And He expects us to be loyal and to worship the God of our fathers when they have been faithful. Personal, religious loyalty to whatever you were born in is, and has been, the cause of much superstitious religious observance, mindlessly repeated over the course of centuries. But it is no solution to rebel against how God made the world, and to try to say that each person must come up with their own Christianity, each generation, from scratch.

In other words, good traditions are good, and bad traditions are bad. But how can we tell? Well, a moment's reflection will show that none of us can get a vantage point from which we can see the whole and make an authoritative decision. This was my earlier point. By myself, I can get no traction. In order to have any confidence at all, I must entrust myself entirely to the grace of God, for He is the only one who can give this gift. Now it happens that I have been born and reared in the Protestant stream of Christendom, which, as it also happens, is the stream which emphasizes the sovereign, gracious, efficacious, overflowing grace of God.

When we baby Protestants grow up to the level of discussion with our friends in Rome where we must produce arguments and scriptural exposition, we do so gladly. But please note that the arguments that I am asking you to consider persuasive are persuasive to *me* because I was loved by parents who lived the life of Christ in the home, and brought up in a church where the gospel was preached and the Scriptures honored and loved. I am, as the dippy poster of a generation ago exhorted me, blooming where I was planted. These are my people, and have been my people for generations. This is not absolute, because there was a point when my Protestant fathers did not walk in the way of their fathers, and they abandoned the idolatry in the mass. And before that, there was a time when my medieval fathers turned from their pagan gods to serve the triune God preached to them by itinerant monks. And they did right in that. Tradition is to be honored and accepted, but never absolutized, and never privileged above the plain statements of the Word of God.

Ah, gotcha, you might think. Plain statements of the Word of God according to *whom*? According to the grace of God mediated to me through all His kindness, and that kindness includes loving parents, faithful and communing churches, open Bibles, and honorable confession. In other words, I am vulnerable and dependent. I am not autonomous, and cannot get free by myself, or off to myself. If I give thanks to God the Father for the Lord Jesus Christ, in the power of the Holy Spirit, and do so in the midst of His congregation, I have every confidence that He will save me. He has promised, and I believe Him. "But what if He doesn't?" somebody asks. Well, if I perish I perish—but I know beyond disputing that if God does not save me, I will certainly not be able to scramble off somewhere else to save myself, or find a savior on my own who will authoritatively bypass my need to trust in Jesus, receiving all His covenant blessings. No, it is all grace, grace upon grace, and grace that saves to the uttermost.

www.ingramcontent.com/pod-product-compliance
Lightning Source LLC
LaVergne TN
LVHW051553080426
835510LV00020B/2962